BudgetYes!

21st Century Solutions
for Taking Control
of Your Money *Now*

What People are saying about BudgetYes!...

"Budgeting is the first step to financial independence. Users of this easy to manage system will be rewarded with more control of their money and more money in their pockets!"

Randy Gardner, LLM, CPA, co-author, 101 Tax Saving Ideas

"I had already tried various budgeting techniques and this information was a fresh perspective."

Rick Hunt, BudgetYes! Graduate

"I found **BudgetYes!** to be easy to read and understand thanks to its simple, friendly language and logical organization. The authors use colorful, fun analogies that crystallize the concepts and realistic examples that clearly demonstrate their budgeting system at work. I think you'll find **BudgetYes!** to be an empowering, stress-relieving tool that puts you in control of your money. The positive effect of this system on your everyday life, your relationships, and your future cannot be underestimated. Give **BudgetYes!** a try!"

Cathy Levy, Software Engineer, Chemical Abstracts Service

"Though usually overlooked, setting up a good personal budget is the first step to any money management activity. Without it, you cannot control your finances and will always fall short of your goals."

Mark J. Randall, CFP, American Express Financial Advisors, Inc.

"I currently use some parts of it, but feel I could go back and implement all of it at anytime. I remember all I was taught and I can't say that about other methods I'd learned!

Linda Robinson, BudgetYes! Graduate

"The concepts introduced in **BudgetYes!** can be used by anyone from student to executive to retiree. It shows how you can take control of your money, rather than a budget controlling you."

Diane Aukland, CPA, James A. Brickweg CPAs

"This personal budgeting system has done several things for me. First, I finally feel in control of our money. When a bill comes the money is already set aside to pay it. Previously, my system consisted of piling up the bills by due date and paying until the money ran out. Now, my husband and I always know how much money we have to spend. ... I am constantly saying to family and friends that this budgeting system has changed my life. They just laugh, but I am totally serious. There is no more worrying about where we'll get the money to pay a bill. ... I am grateful that this budgeting system has shown me how to take control of my family's finances."

Angela Pryce, BudgetYes! Graduate

BudgetYes!

21st Century Solutions
for Taking Control
of Your Money *Now*

by
Jane E. Chidester
John L. Macko

TULIPTREE
•P•R•E•S•S•

Columbus, Ohio

BudgetYes!™

21ˢᵗ Century Solutions for Taking Control of Your Money *Now*

by
Jane E. Chidester
John L. Macko

Tulip Tree Press
P.O. Box 1495-2
Powell, Ohio 43065

Disclaimer: Although the publisher and authors have exhaustively researched all sources to ensure accuracy and completeness of the information contained in this book, there may be both typographical and content mistakes. We shall have neither liability nor responsibility to any person or entity with respect to any loss or damage caused, or alleged to be caused, directly or indirectly by the information contained in this book. It is sold with the understanding that the publisher and authors are not engaged in rendering legal, accounting, or other professional services. If expert assistance is required, the services of a competent professional should be sought. If you do not wish to be bound by the above, you may return this book for a full refund.

Publisher's Cataloging in Publication Data
Chidester, Jane E., 1962-

> BudgetYes! 21ˢᵗ Century Solutions for Taking Control of Your Money *Now*
> /Jane E. Chidester and John L. Macko.– 1ˢᵗ ed.
> 224p. illus. cm.
> Includes index.
> ISBN 0-9655198-3-X: $19.95
> 1. Finance, Personal.   I. Macko, John L. jt. auth. II. Title.
> 2. Budgets, Household.
> HG179.C56 1997 332.024
> Library of Congress Catalog Card Number: 97-90123

Attention Colleges and Universities, Corporations, and Professional Organizations: Quantity discounts are available on bulk purchases of this book for educational training purposes, fund raising, or gift giving. Special books, booklets, or book excerpts can also be created to fit your specific needs. For information contact the publisher listed above. Thank you!

Printed on acid free paper with soy ink.

Table of Contents

Dear Readers

Acknowledgments

Chapter 1: Why Budget?   1

What is in it for you?   2

What is a budget?   2

Seven Benefits of Budgeting   2

Three Common Misconceptions about Budgeting   4

Summary   6

Chapter 2: Why BudgetYes?   7

Three Other Budgeting Systems   7

The Ideas Behind the BudgetYes System   9

The BudgetYes Philosophy   11

How this Book is Organized   12

What you need to Start   12

Summary   14

Chapter 3: Identifying Your Expenses   15

How to Make a List   15

Decide on Budget Items   16

Organize Your Records   18

Summary   18

Chapter 4: Identifying Your Income   19

Income Events   20

How to Normalize Income Events   20

Use a Savings and Checking Account Together   22

Money Received More than Four Times a Month   22

Money Received Less than 12 Times a Year   22

Other Options to Normalize your Income Events   24

The Difference Between Income and Bonuses   25

Summary   26

Chapter 5: The Heart of BudgetYes   27
The Master Budget Sheet   29
Income Events Reserve Budgeted Amounts   29
Spending Budgeted Money   30
How to Mark Boxes   30
How many Master Budget Sheets?   32
Summary   32

Chapter 6: Your Spending Money   33
The "$" Account is a Virtual Account   33
Your Refunds, Gifts, and Bonuses Go Here!   34
The "$" Account is also a Buffer   34
A Budget Snapshot—For You and Others   37
Summary   37

Chapter 7: Types of Budget Items   39
Simple Budget Items   40
Bounded Budget Items   44
Picking the Amount for the Bounded Item   44
No History of Past Bills?   46
Working With Your Chosen Amount   46
Monitored Budget Items   47
Picking the Amount for the Monitored Item   51
Summary   53

Chapter 8: Putting It All Together   55
Income and Deductions   56
Picking Budget Items and Amounts   57
Setting up the Budget   58
BudgetYes Sheets for Sample Family Budget   61
Starting the Budget   63
Summary   64

Chapter 9: Running BudgetYes   65
Example: Money Enters the Budget   67
Example: Spending Unbudgeted Money   72
Example: Simple Budget Item   73

Example: Bills Prior to Budget Start Date 75
Example: Processing Your Bank Statement 78
Example: Monitored Budget Item 80
Example: Next Income Event 82
Example: Bounded Budget Item & Multiple Bills 84
Summary 87

Chapter 10: Exercises 89
Summary 90

Chapter 11: Answers to Exercises 91
Final State of the Budget, After the Exercises 94
Summary 99

Chapter 12: Three Month Example Budget 101
Summary 108

Chapter 13: Reconciling 109
The Mechanics of Reconciliation 110
Four Steps to Reconciling Your Budget 111
A Reconciliation Example 111
Things That Go Wrong 117
How Strict Should You Be? 121
Mark Your Reconciliation Points! 122
How Often Should You Reconcile? 123
Summary 124

Chapter 14: Changes to Your Budget 125
Begin Again 125
Phase in New Master Budget Sheets 126
Making Minor Adjustments 126
Monitored Budget Account Transfers 128
Save Old Budget Sheets 130
Automatic Adjustments: Raises and Bonuses 130
The Magnificent Triple 131
Summary 133

Chapter 15: Your Money Habits   **135**

Using Cash   136
Using Credit Cards   138
Important Point about Credit Card Usage   138
What to Look for in a Credit Card   141
How to Handle Credit Card Purchases   141
Overlaying Investment Accounts   145
Income Event Normalization   147
Summary   148

Chapter 16: Budgeting on a Computer   **149**

Seven Advantages of Computers   149
Commercial Software   151
Difference Between Software and BudgetYes   152
How to Handle the Difference   153
Creating Your Own System   153
Summary   154

Chapter 17: Where Do You Go From Here?   **155**

Written Goals   156
Take Advantage of Money Management Tips   158
Plan for Retirement   159
Three Benefits of Automatic Payments   162
Pay Yourself After Repaying Loans   163
Pay Yourself With Windfalls   165
Use Your Budget for Self-improvement   165
Summary   166

Chapter 18: Final Thought   **167**

Appendix A (Master Budget Sheet)
Appendix B (Monitored Account Sheet)
Appendix C (List of Possible Budget Items)
Index
About the Authors
Questionnaire
Order Forms

Dear Readers,

Things happen so quickly!

Throughout our childhoods, early educational experiences, and even college years, our focus was to learn a job so that we could get out in the "real" world and make money. And sure enough, before we knew what had happened, we found ourselves earning a salary, with monthly rent, a car payment, utility bills, and the need to pay for groceries, gasoline, and unexpected expenses. There had been no plan: it all just happened somehow.

We decided to take the bull by the horns, and committed to implement an, *ugh*, budget.

Of course, this was not a new idea. Our parents and mentors had been telling us to budget all along. They just never told us *how*. No one ever offered any instructions, suggestions, or explanations. It was as if everyone assumed that creating a budget was some innate human ability, not unlike, we supposed, stubbing our toe or hitting our thumb with a hammer.

So, off to the library and bookstores we went. There were a few "how to budget" books, but they were either trivial to the point of uselessness, or else contained an endless progression of forms to fill out and computations to make, with questionable results.

Putting bits and pieces together from here and there, we began to learn about what budgets were supposed to do, what they were good for, and how they were supposed to work. What we wanted was a system that would give us the tools to control our money, monitor how we were progressing in terms of our plans and goals, and still not be inordinately time-consuming to run on a weekly basis.

So, little by little, our budgeting system was born. We took all the good ideas we could find, got rid of the "busy work", and added little touches of our own. We ran this budget for over a decade, tweaking wherever we could to make it more powerful and easier to use.

As family members made their official entrances into the "real world", they quickly encountered the same frustrations about budgeting that we had. We shared our system with them, and they told us they liked it!

Based on these experiences, we wanted to share what we had learned outside our circle of relatives, not only to help others, but also as a way to make a contribution to our community. Using our skills in education, particularly course work dealing with making learning fun, we created a Personal Budgeting class, and about five years ago began teaching it through various Parks and Recreation Programs around the city. For a traditionally "dull" topic, it became one of the most popular (and in one program *the* most popular) offerings. Many people started requesting the material in book form, and hence this project was born. As you'll see from the testimonials and acknowledgments, former students gave valuable feedback and help in reviewing our manuscript. The heartwarming responses amazed and touched us, inspiring us on to reach an even larger audience.

One of the biggest challenges we had was choosing a name for all of this. Unfortunately, most people have grown to hate the word "budget." Try this experiment on your friends. Walk up to them and say that word and notice the expression on their faces. Then say terms like "root canal", "tetanus shot", and "spinal tap." Notice that the expressions will remain unchanged.

For us, a budget is a tool we genuinely *value*. No, we don't prefer sitting in front of our checkbook to, say, a walk in the woods or a vacation. However, we find the planning and control tools indispensable, love the way that bill-paying time has been converted from a mindset of losing money to gaining money (more about this in later chapters), and would no sooner give it up than other basic tools such as our oven or lawnmower. We wanted to say it like it is, without sugar coating, and prove that running a budget is something to be proud of and positive about. We could think of no more positive word in the English language than "yes", so we glued that on to the concept we were trying to promote, and hence the name BudgetYes.

> **budget,** *noun*
> **1. a.** An itemized summary of estimated or intended expenditures for a given period along with proposals for financing them **b.** A systematic plan for the expenditure of a usually fixed resource, such as money or time, during a given period **c.** The total sum of money allocated for a particular purpose or period of time.
> **budget,** *verb*
> **1.** To plan in advance the expenditure of.

So did we invent this budgeting system? Well, yes and no. Mostly no. As the old saying goes, there's nothing new under the sun. BudgetYes is a collection of what to us are the very best budgeting ideas collected from other budgeting systems, computer systems and accounting programs, and hundreds of students and friends. Yes, we've added some ideas of our own and tried to improve existing practices. But our main contribution, we hope, is to present everything in a clear, organized, and enjoyable fashion, and to save you the years of trial and error that it took to work all this out for ourselves.

All this is not to say that you can't customize your own budget. On the contrary, this book is organized into building blocks, encouraging you to make your budget a tool you will genuinely value, as we do.

Using a budget to guide the use of your money is the most fundamental, most critical aspect of a person's financial life. Without knowing how your spending compares to your income, you cannot even start a savings plan. When most people think about "money management" or "financial management", what they really mean is how to make smart investment decisions for their savings. You can't even *think* about this step if you have not done the *first* step, which is budgeting.

This book starts out, in Chapter 1, with the reasons for budgeting and examples of some of the benefits you can expect to gain if you do budget faithfully. We found that keeping these benefits firmly in mind gave us the motivation and discipline to stick to our money plan, and soon, running our budget was second nature.

Chapter 2 looks at the main features of other budgeting systems, and shows how the BudgetYes system incorporates the best of each. In our early experiments with budgets, we quickly learned that a basic necessity is knowing how much money you have and what it is earmarked for. When you look at your checkbook balance and see a total, how much of that money is for groceries? How much for entertainment? How much can you spend for clothing? Chapter 2 goes on to introduce the concept of an overlay, showing how you can gain detailed knowledge of how you've allocated your expenditures.

Basic to any budget are income and expenditures. Put in the vernacular, how much money is comin' in, and how much is goin' out? Chapters 3 and 4 look at these important topics. Discussed are tracking methods for expenses; how to decide on what items you should budget for; deciding whether you should budget on a weekly, biweekly, or monthly basis; and how to smooth out any income variances you may experience throughout the year.

Recall that one of our early frustrations with other budgeting systems was that they required you to fill out form after form after form. We knew it didn't have to be that complicated, and resolved to prove it. BudgetYes only uses *two* forms. The first of these is presented in Chapter 5, and is the heart of the system. The Master Budget Sheet is the tool you can use to visually map your earnings to your wants and needs. This simple form puts your plans into action, and dynamically ensures that you will have the exact amounts of money available for the purposes you decide.

The other form is introduced in Chapter 6, and may well turn out to be your favorite budgeting feature. This simple accounting sheet is the "shock absorber" of the system, smoothing out the peaks and valleys. But really, this form is used as a place to accumulate spending money. In fact, in many ways BudgetYes is geared toward optimizing "extra" money for you, and this simple accounting device is what makes this all possible.

Chapter 7 examines the various types of items you can budget for. As you probably already know from experience, bills can vary widely as to their "predictability". Some bills are exactly the same month in and month out. Others can vary widely; seasonal variations and other circumstances can produce staggering differences that just aren't fun to discover in your mailbox. Fortunately, there is good news. The same simple form introduced in Chapter 6 can impart predictability to the madness.

The basics out of the way, the next four chapters cover examples, examples, and more examples. Following the antics of a hypothetical family, Chapter 8 shows all the necessary steps to set up a budget. Chapter 9 then shows the BudgetYes system in action, week by week, day by day, and bill by bill. For those who like to learn by doing, Chapter 10 presents some exercises to try, with the answers spelled out in detail in Chapter 11. Finally, Chapter 12 presents a complete three-month example of a completed budgeting system.

The process of reconciling is explained in Chapter 13. Reconciling helps you to find errors within your budget, and ensures your budget amounts are in synch with reality.

Things change. Chapter 14 explains how to keep your budget current with the inevitable transitions that will occur.

Budgets are as individual and unique as the people who create and use them. As mentioned a few paragraphs back, BudgetYes encourages custom modifications. Do you prefer using cash over checks? Do you feel more comfortable just carrying a wad of "mad money" around? Do you use a set of plastic cards for many different types of purchases? Could you benefit from a special "budget" from your investments? Check out Chapter 15. For those who want to use a computer to help with the budgeting and bill paying, Chapter 16 offers even more ideas.

Finally, Chapters 17 and 18 leave you with some final thoughts of things to try once your budget is up and running. It's our hope that you can build on your budgeting successes to create even more successes in your life.

We genuinely want you to succeed, and to be able to run a budgeting system that will be a valuable tool in reaching your financial goals. And we hope you have some fun in the process. These wishes encapsulate the reasons we wrote this book.

Yes, things happen quickly. Success with a budget can be one of those things.

Best wishes to you and what we hope is your soon-to-be great success with BudgetYes!

Jane and John
June 1997

P.S. We would love to know what you think of BudgetYes. There is a questionnaire in the back of the book, but any thought you would be so kind as to share with us would be most welcome. If your idea or comments are used in a future edition, your name will be listed in the acknowledgments section, and you will receive a free copy.

You can't run away
from trouble, there
ain't no place that far.

A sign in the
Splash Mountain Attraction
at Disneyland
and Walt Disney World

Acknowledgments

We would like to thank the following individuals, without whom this work would not have been possible:

Our parents, siblings, and other relatives, for their love and constant support.

Mr. Jeff Card, of *Dublin Parks and Recreation*, for the opportunity to present our first budgeting seminar.

The many students of our **BudgetYes!** seminars, who not only encouraged us to write this book, but also whose every question and suggestion made this system better and easier to understand and use.

We would also like to thank the following individuals who tirelessly reviewed our manuscript before it went to press. These people helped shape and organize this book into what it is today.

Diane C. Aukland, *Certified Public Accountant, James A. Brickweg Certified Public Accountants*

Carolyn Anson, *CPA, Pricing Analyst, Chemical Abstract Service*

J. Mark Anson, *Senior Systems Engineer, Chemical Abstracts Service*

O. Jay Armstrong, *Service Manager, Gras & Sons*

Barbara Chidester, *R.N., M.A.*

Mary Chidester, *Paralegal, Law Firm of Vorys, Sater, Seymour, and Pease*

Greg Forst, *BudgetYes! Graduate*

Rick Hunt, *BudgetYes! Graduate*

Cathy Levy, *Software Engineer Chemical Abstracts Service*

Angela Pryce, *BudgetYes! Graduate*

Mark J. Randall, *Certified Financial Planner, American Express Financial Advisors, Inc.*

Janet Rogers, *BudgetYes! Graduate*

Jeffrey Sheban, *Business Reporter, The Columbus Dispatch*

Barbara H. Smith, *Plain City, OH*

Mike Strapp, *BudgetYes! Graduate*

Christi and Brian Young, *BudgetYes! Graduates*

BudgetYes!

21st Century Solutions
for Taking Control
of Your Money *Now*

The best place to
start is where you
are with what you
have.

Charles Schwab

1

Why Budget?

A budget is the most fundamental and most effective financial management tool available to anyone.

Yes, anyone—whether you are earning thousands of dollars a year, or hundreds of thousands of dollars. It is extremely important to know how much money you have to spend, and where you are spending it. Yes, some of your "spending" might be for investments, but there is an important distinction between creating a personal budget and deciding where to *invest* your extra income. A budget is the first and most important step towards maximizing the power of your money.

What is in it for you?

Just about everything. A carpenter would never start work on a new house without a blueprint. An aerospace firm would never begin construction on a new rocket booster without a detailed set of design specifications. Yet many of us find ourselves in the circumstance of getting out on our own and making, spending, and investing money without a plan to guide us.

Budgeting is about planning. And planning is crucial to produce a desired result.

What is a budget?

A budget is a money plan. With it, you can organize and control your financial resources, set and realize goals, and decide in advance how your money will work for you. A budget can be as simple as it is powerful.

The basic idea behind budgeting is to save money *up front* for both known and unknown expenses.

Seven Benefits of Budgeting

So what benefits, specifically, can you expect if you set up a budget? Naturally, the answer to this question will be different for everyone. But here are some of the most common benefits that people see when they start a budget:

Knowing what is going on. Personal budgeting allows you to know exactly how much money you have—even down to the penny, if you so desire. Furthermore, a budget is a self-education tool that shows you how your funds are allocated, how they are working for you, what your plans are for them, and how far along you are toward reaching your goals. "Knowledge is power," as the oft-quoted saying of George Eliot goes, and knowing about your money is the first step toward controlling it. That leads us to our next benefit:

Control. A budget is the key to enabling you to take charge of your finances. With a budget, you have the tools to decide exactly what is going to happen to your hard-earned money—and when. You can be in control of your money, instead of having your money limit what you do. *This bears repeating: you can be in control of your money, instead of letting it control you!*

Organization. Even in its simplest form, a budget systematizes, or divides, funds into categories of expenditures and savings. Beyond that, however, budgets can provide further organization by automatically providing records of all your monetary transactions. They can also provide the foundation for a simple filing system to organize bills, receipts, and financial statements.

Communication. If you are married, have a family, or share money with anyone, having a budget that you both (or all) create together is a key to resolving personal differences about money handling. The budget is a communication tool to discuss the priorities for where your money should be spent, as well as enabling all involved parties to "run" the system.

Take advantage of opportunities. Knowing the exact state of your personal monetary affairs, and being in control of them, allows you to take advantage of opportunities that you might otherwise miss. Have you ever wondered if you could afford something? With a budget, you will never have to wonder again—you will know.

Extra time. All your financial transactions are automatically organized for tax time, for creditor questions, in fact, for any query which may come up regarding how and when you spent money. Being armed with such information sure saves time digging through old records.

Extra money. This might well be everyone's favorite benefit. A budget will almost certainly produce extra money for you to do with as you wish. Hidden fees and lost interest paid to outsiders can be eliminated forever. Unnecessary expenditures, once identified, can be stripped out. Savings, even small ones, can be accumulated and made to *work* for you.

Three Common Misconceptions about Budgeting

Many people never even consider starting a budget because they are afraid they will have to "give up" something. To some, a budget is like a diet that may force them to forgo a favorite treat. In our experience, a diet is the wrong metaphor to use when thinking about budgeting.

Myth #1: You have to suffer to use a budget. The truth is, you are following a budget whether or not you have consciously implemented one. Unfortunately, the "budget" you end up with by doing nothing is almost certainly an endless cycle of reactions, as opposed to a dynamic, proactive strategy. A reactive mode contains the double whammy of the anxiety of wondering when the money will run out, and then feeling deprived when it does. A budget will actually *reduce* your suffering.

A more accurate analogy than a diet is a cluttered hall closet. You know the one—a closet you are afraid to open lest you be hit on the head by a cascade of falling junk. The one everyone puts things into, but never takes anything out of. The one that prompted a scientist at the local university to schedule an archeological dig.

Picture that closet in your mind for a moment. Now imagine taking everything out and laying it all on the floor where you can see it and study it. Then, give the closet a thorough cleaning, and perhaps install some new shelves or racks inside. Finally, put everything back in an organized, neat arrangement. Do you know what? You will have more storage room than when you started—and you did not get rid of anything.

Now, it might well be that when you have all the junk on the floor, you decide you can probably do without the muddy pair of galoshes with the holes in the bottom, or the broken baseball bat, or the jigsaw puzzle with half the pieces missing. If you get rid of some items, you have even more room in the closet.

A budget works the same way. *The very act of organizing your finances can provide extra money!* During the organization process, you might discover some expenses you want to eliminate, or some smarter ways of handling payments. These choices give you more money still.

Myth #2: You have to be in debt to budget. Another popular misconception is that budgets are only for people who are in real financial trouble—individuals who are severely in debt or currently living way beyond their means. While it is true such circumstances require a budget overhaul (or, more likely, implementation), the truth is that *everyone* can benefit from budgeting.

Successful companies, operating solidly in the black and generating millions of dollars in annual revenue, all maintain budgets. Some companies have entire departments, with dozens of employees, whose sole purpose is to run the budgeting process. These companies don't do all of this because they are in financial trouble or are spending beyond their means. They do it because budgets *work*.

Yes, a budget can be the road to financial recovery from a crisis. But it can also lead to even more organization, control and wealth building if your current financial situation is on the upswing.

Myth #3: You have to spend extra hours doing paperwork. Another common fear is that budgeting will take inordinate amounts of time. With some older budgeting systems, this is certainly true. Even with the newer systems, there is certainly an investment of time up front to get things rolling. But with the BudgetYes system, which will be explained in detail within this book, it can be as simple as checking a box every time you write a check.

Summary

A budget is the most fundamental and most effective money management tool available to anyone. Whether your income is salary, hourly, commission, tip, investment, or self-employment based, you can be in control of your money, and make it work for you. Budgets need not be complex, time consuming, or demanding. The very act of organizing your finances can provide extra money by showing you where the leaks in your system are!

2

Why BudgetYes?

BudgetYes is designed to give you the full power and benefits of a sophisticated budgeting system, and yet be easy to use. To understand the advantages of BudgetYes, and how it simplifies the budgeting process, let's look at the workings of some other popular systems.

Three Other Budgeting Systems

The envelope method. This system has been around for a long time and has been used by many people. The idea behind this method is to use envelopes to divide your pay into categories, with each category targeted toward a specific expense. To use this system, you would obtain a stack of envelopes, and decide what expenses you wanted to budget for: for example, car payments, telephone bills, monthly rent, and so on. Then, one envelope would be allocated for each expense, and you would write the amount of the expense on the front of the envelope. Come payday, you would put the appropriate amount in each envelope. The money would then stay in the envelopes until the time came to pay the corresponding bill, at which point the funds would be taken out and used.

The basic ideas behind this system are good ones: money is reserved "up front" for expenses and discipline is enforced in following an established budget. The major problem with this method, of course, is that it was designed for a time when most transactions were handled in cash. People received pay envelopes containing bills and coins, and the folding green stuff exchanged hands for most purchases and payments.

In today's world of checks, credit cards, and electronic banking, such a system is a nightmare. You would spend an enormous amount of time making cash withdrawals and deposits. Safety is another concern. Can't you just picture someone breaking into your home to find a collection of delicious, money-filled envelopes to choose from? Even worse is the fact that money sitting around in envelopes isn't *working* for you. Instead of just laying there, gathering dust, you want those funds out there making more money.

The "wish list" method. This system can be simply described as "good intentions, bad results." The basic scenario here is that a family sits down and agrees on "spending limits" for certain categories of household expenses. "We won't spend any more than $450 a month on groceries" they might say. All of these decisions are carefully documented on paper. That done, the list is carefully filed away, and the family goes out and begins their spending.

The problem here is there is no easy way to enforce the budget plan. When someone takes a trip to the grocery store, they have no idea how much they are "allowed" to spend. Furthermore, rarely do grocery bills come out to exactly $450 a month. If the family spends under that amount, the extra is never seen or heard from again. If they go over budget, where does the extra money come from? Soon, the frustration of not being in control of the situation sets in, and the list is forgotten.

The "list-in-the-pocket" method. This system is an attempt to put some control on the "wish-list" method. Instead of filing the "wish list" away, the family carries it around in pocket, purse, or wallet. Then, every time some money is spent, the amount is deducted from the appropriate category. With this technique, some feedback is available as to how things are going.

But still, there are problems. What does the family do if they need gasoline, and there is no money left in the gasoline budget? What if both husband and wife happen to stop at the grocery store while running separate errands? Do they carry separate budget lists? Do they have to spend time reconciling their lists at the end of the day?

Perhaps the biggest annoyance with this type of system is the constant attention it requires. Imagine being at a soda machine, and needing to pull out and make entries on a list before you can deposit a few coins! What a pain.

The Ideas Behind the BudgetYes System

BudgetYes takes the best ideas from many budgeting systems and adds quite a few of its own. It is designed to let you divide and reserve your funds, and remain in control of them, without a lot of extra work. It allows easy transfer of funds among budgeted items so you won't starve if you happen to run out of grocery money. And it provides a single reconciliation point so that all family members can use a single budget plan.

BudgetYes works through the concept of an overlay. This overlay allows you to see the way your funds are divided up and reserved for special purposes—*it imparts organization to your finances without changing them or the way you handle them.*

To illustrate this idea, suppose you were given an aerial photograph of a town that you had never visited, and asked to pick out a few locations of interest: the park at the corner of Elm and Main, or the bank at High and Third. Pretty tough assignment, right? Now, suppose you were handed an overlay printed on celluloid—that clear plastic material used for overhead projector transparencies and animation drawings. A map of the city, with all the streets clearly marked, would be printed on the celluloid. Placing the map on top of the photograph, you could pick out that park and bank with ease! Notice that the photograph itself would not change at all, but your understanding of it would be significantly enhanced with the use of the overlay.

BudgetYes works hand-in-hand with your checking account to provide an overlay of your checking account balance. Normally, when you look at the final line of your checkbook balance, you don't have much of a clue as to what that money is for. How much of it can you spend on groceries? How much do you need to reserve for all your utility bills? The BudgetYes overlay system will give you those details. You will always know the disposition of every penny, all without changing your checkbook, the way you pay bills, or the way you write checks.

Another idea central to the BudgetYes system is that it allows you to focus your attention where you need to. The daily, routine assaults on your checkbook as you pay monthly bills and take care of mundane expenses can get in the way of truly managing your money and concentrating on financial strategies.

A good analogy here might be to put you in sole charge of a day-care center responsible for 20 active four-year-olds. To add complication, suppose that one child had a special need that day—perhaps she had suddenly become ill and required lots of special attention. Stranded by yourself, this situation would be very difficult to deal with. But what if you could enlist some helpers? Suppose you could call in additional workers to watch the other children while you administered the special care. You could devote your attention where it was needed.

The BudgetYes system can be your helper to handle all the routine aspects of your income and payments, *allowing you to concentrate on the important things: investments, savings, financial growth, important purchases, or whatever your priorities are.*

The BudgetYes Philosophy

Besides the basic concepts just discussed, there is one very important philosophy behind the BudgetYes system:

> ## A budget is a tool, not a dictator.

This means that a budget is something you should use to control your finances. It is *not* something that should control you.

Even the best-organized and most well-intentioned budget will experience setbacks from time to time. Family emergencies, medical needs, and unfortunate disasters are some of the types of unexpected expenses that, sooner or later, we all run into. Yes, a good budget can be used to plan for many of these calamities. But the point is that if you are intelligent enough to set up and use a budget in the first place, you also have the wherewithal to know when to take the thing off auto pilot and drive it yourself.

How this Book is Organized

The chapters of this book will provide explanations of basic building blocks that you can use to set up your personalized budget. Exercises and examples along the way will help you get comfortable with each idea. Some of the ideas will appeal to you. Great—use 'em. Some of the ideas you may not like at all. That's fine too—ignore those. Some of the ideas may lead you to even better ideas of your own, and that's wonderful.[1] The objective is for you to take all the building blocks you end up with and use them to construct a highly customized (not complicated!) financial tool tailored to your needs.

When should you actually begin to set up your own budget? Should you read this entire book first, or should you begin working on your budget as you read along? The authors recommend that you read to at least Chapter 9, which provides a summary of the basic steps to set up your budget. By then, you'll be familiar with most of the concepts and building blocks.

What you need to Start

✓ **A few photocopies of the sheets in Appendices A and B.**

✓ **A pencil and an eraser.** (The eraser is optional if you never make mistakes! ☺)

---

[1]By the way, if you do come up with some great ideas for use within the BudgetYes system, please consider sending them to us. We would love to share your ideas with others in future editions of this book. Send to Tulip Tree Press, P. O. Box 1495-2, Powell, Ohio 43065

✓ **A calculator.** (This isn't absolutely essential—we ran this budget for several years doing all our calculations on scratch paper!) Chances are good that you or your family already have at least one calculator laying around somewhere. Even the simplest of calculators will be more than adequate for running a household budget. However, if you happen to be considering the purchase of a new calculator, we recommend considering a financial calculator that allows computations involving time, money, and interest. Such a calculator can answer questions like:

"If I put $100 in an account every month and earn 8% interest, how much money will be in the account when I retire at age 65?"

or

"If I want to borrow $125,000 for a house, and the bank is currently offering a 10% rate for a 30-year loan, what will my monthly payments be?"

You might find such a calculator invaluable for your future financial planning. Most of these calculators come with detailed instruction manuals and lots of examples.

✓ **An interest-bearing checking account.** In reality, any checking account will work just fine with the BudgetYes system. As you will soon see, however, the budgeting system you are learning automatically reserves money for expenses until you write a check. You want those reserved funds working for you, and that is why we suggest an interest-bearing account.

It may be that you have postponed getting an interest-bearing account because the financial institutions in your area charge a fee, or require a minimum average balance, for such an account. If this is the case, set up your budget using your current checking account, and then monitor your average monthly balance closely. You will probably find that because of the new way you're handling your money, an interest-bearing account will be a profitable move.

✓ **Records of your past income and expenditures.** These will be identified and explained as necessary.

Summary

BudgetYes works hand-in-hand with your checking account to provide an overlay of your checking account balance. This allows you to focus your attention where it is needed. A budget is a tool. It is a vehicle you can use to watch over your money and have the flexibility to make the best spending decisions possible.

3

Identifying Your Expenses

The first step in setting up your budget is to simply identify where your money is going at present. It is time to rummage through that cluttered hall closet, as described in Chapter 1. Open the door and take a look, take everything out and spread it in front of you, and write down what you see.

How to Make a List

A good starting point for determining where your money is going is to itemize those things that you write checks for, or pay, on a monthly basis. Your checkbook register and credit card statements will probably provide these records: rent or house payment, telephone bills, grocery expenses, electricity and/or natural gas bills, and so on. Create a base list of the standard expenses that you know you will have month in and month out.

With that step done, add to the list those categories of items you've spent money on during the last few months. Perhaps even go back a year. This exercise should uncover expenses that do not occur regularly every month such as vacations, unexpected car repairs, insurance premiums, holiday gifts, and tax payments.

Do not overwhelm yourself when making this list, but do take a serious look just to see how you've spent your money over the last year. The very act of doing this step will give you tremendous benefits even if you go no further. Stopping to reflect on purchases and spending habits will help you make better decisions in the future. Paraphrasing one of the benefits mentioned in Chapter 1, *the very act of organizing your expenses can provide extra money*!

For these steps, some people find it helpful to carry a pad and pencil around with them to keep track of their expenses. While this isn't something you want to do for the rest of your life, when you're just starting to get a handle on your expenses it can be a very useful and enlightening exercise. This is particularly helpful for tracking cash expenditures, for which no other written record may be available.

Decide on Budget Items

The next step is to take your list of expenses and start thinking about what items you'll initially include in your budget. Avoid the temptation to make your list too complicated in the beginning. Pick out the items that are large expenditures, or that you routinely pay on a regular basis, or that you feel would do you the most good to track. You can start small and add to your budgeted items as you gain experience and as you understand your needs better.

Even budgeting for a few items will help. A budget of only ten or fifteen items is not unusual, and you might be pleasantly surprised at the positive effects that monitoring just a few items will have. The key here is the *focusing* of your attention that was described in Chapter 2. The BudgetYes system can be your helper to handle all the routine aspects of your income and payments, allowing you to concentrate on the important things.

See Appendix C for a list of possible expense categories. A long list is presented to try to cover all the bases—everyone has different needs and different expenditures they may want to watch.

 TIP: Make sure to include budgeting for a "fun" item, such as a vacation, CD player, or some luxury item you'd really like to have. Having a "fun" goal will really motivate you to stick with your new goals.

Involve family members and significant others in the selection of the budgeted items and the design of the budget itself. Setting up a budget is an excellent communication tool that will allow all expenses to be laid out clearly for comparison, discussion, and analysis. It should come as no surprise that finances are the most common source of conflict in the household.[2] Not only are disagreements about money handling the top reason couples fight, but also it is the leading cause of divorce! Laying all expenses out on the table at once makes decisions easier. It is also easier to agree on a budget once than to agonize over spending decisions

---

[2] Money is the #1 source of conflict in the household, according to many sources, including the October 1994 issue of *American Demographics*, page 11. The study reported in the article, Money and Marital Discord, was conducted by Roper Starch Worldwide for *Worth* Magazine. *JET* reported in their November 18, 1996 issue, in the article Why Money is the Leading Cause of Divorce(p. 34), that 57% of divorced couples cited money problems as the cause (survey done by Citibank).

month in and month out. Involving children in the discussions can be a very positive experience as well. They can learn the value of money, understand why spending limits are necessary, and appreciate the value of planning at an early age.

Organize Your Records

Another of the benefits of budgeting mentioned in Chapter 1 is that setting up your budget provides a foundation for getting your financial records organized. Do you ever go hunting for that car title, old receipt, or past bills? Do you just throw your monthly statements in a box or paper bag when you are done paying bills? Does the stack of old papers just keep growing higher on your desk or kitchen counter? Though sometimes a daunting task initially, organizing your records will save you time, and time again.

Whatever your preference: filing cabinet, accordion file, plastic or cardboard box—a single, convenient location, large enough to accommodate additions is crucial to an efficient record keeping system. Important original documents (contracts, certificates, licenses, deeds) should be stored in a safe-deposit box or fireproof strongbox. It is a good idea to keep *copies* of these important originals in your home files.

Summary

Just the act of identifying your expenses and writing them down can give you indispensable insights into where your money is going, where you can and should cut back, where problem areas exist and where opportunities might be. For some people, just getting to this point can have a revolutionary effect on their finances. But please don't stop here—there are lots of other benefits to come!

4

Identifying Your Income

After identifying your expenses, the next step in setting up your budget is to decide how often—and when—money will come in to the budget.

If you receive a regular paycheck, then money comes into your budget on your payday. However, this is not always the case.. For example, some people in emergency situations temporarily need to live off their savings. Others derive some or all of their income from investments. Others get most of their earnings from tips (gratuities), often on a daily basis. For all of these cases, there is no payday per se. Individuals in these situations either have to decide when money will enter their budget, or take some specific action to move the money there, or both. When you put money into your budget, it's called an *Income Event*.

> An *Income Event* occurs when money is put into a
> budget. An Income Event is always associated
> with a specific date.

Income Events

Now, you may be reading the above definition and thinking to
yourself, "Well, this sounds like a payday to me! Why do we
need a fancy term like 'Income Event'? Why can't we just call it
a payday?"

Most of the time, an Income Event and a payday will be exactly
the same, but because of the exceptions noted above, we'll use
"Income Event" to specifically mean when money enters a
budget.

How to Normalize Income Events

To use the BudgetYes system effectively, you must "normalize"
your Income Events to between one and four per month. Said
another way, money should be put into your budget somewhere
between once a week and once a month. Less frequently than
this does not provide enough control. More frequently than this
leads to too much accounting and paperwork, and you have better things to do with your time.

To *normalize* means to make regular, or consistent. To normalize your income means to figure out what your minimum monthly income is, and "deposit" it into your budget in consistent and regular amounts. As mentioned, "depositing" between one and four times per month is best, depending on the degree of control you'd like to have.

For most people, this requirement is already taken care of. For most, an Income Event is a payday, and most people get their pay twice a month. So, if you get paid every other Wednesday, or every other Friday, or on the 1st and the 15th, or the 15th and the 30th, you're done. You have *two* Income Events per month.

You are also in good shape if your money comes in once a month or once a week.

If your circumstances are different, we are going to use a trick to make it look to your budget as though you are "paid" either once, twice, or four times per month.

Classic examples of individuals in this situation are waitresses, waiters, and taxicab drivers who receive a large portion of their income as tips on a daily basis. Here, there can be over 20 Income Events per month, well over the prescribed limit. Salespersons who receive frequent commissions are in this same situation, as are individuals who are in business for themselves who may get paid at the completion of a job, sale, or other business transaction.

On the other end of the scale are teachers and seasonal workers who may elect not to work for some portion of the year. A teacher, for example, may have the summer off and hence only

receive income for eight or nine months—income that has to
stretch to cover all twelve months.

Use a Savings and Checking Account Together

A simple way to "normalize" these situations is to use a savings
account in conjunction with your checking account. Put money
into the savings account as you receive it, and transfer it to your
checking account (and hence your budget) as you need it.

Money Received More than Four Times a Month

Suppose you receive tips every day and want to normalize this
pay to one Income Event per month. You would deposit your
tips, as frequently as you wished, into your savings account.
Then, once a month, you would transfer money to your checking account, and that would be your "payday"—your Income
Event.

Money Received Less than 12 Times a Year

What about the seasonal worker who has no income for some
months of the year? Here, the savings account is used to retain
money until it is needed.

Suppose a person worked eight months of the year, and for each
of those eight months received a take-home pay of $2,345.67.
Multiplying that figure by 8 shows us that her take-home pay for
the entire year would be $18,765.36. Dividing that number by 12
(the number of months in a year) shows us that her effective
monthly pay is $1,563.78. Hence, for each of the eight months
she is paid, our seasonal worker would place $1,563.78 into her

checking account and budget, and place the remaining $781.89 ($2,345.67 minus $1,563.78) into her savings account. At the end of her work year, she would have $6,255.12 saved up (8 times $781.89), which would allow exactly four withdrawals of her normal monthly income of $1,563.78 to cover the remaining months of the year. This is shown graphically below.

Actual Monthly pay × 8 = Annual pay
        ($2,345.67 × 8 = $18,765.36)

Annual pay ÷ 12 = Effective Monthly pay
        ($18,765.36 ÷ 12 = $1,563.78)

Actual Monthly pay − Effective Monthly pay = Savings
        ($2,345.67 − $1,563.78 = $781.89)

Savings × 8 = Effective Monthly pay for 4 months
        ($781.89 × 8 = $6,255.12 = $1,563.78 × 4)

✓ **NOTE:** The above analysis ignores the fact that savings accounts pay interest. If the savings account used pays 5% interest, and if 8 deposits were put in and 4 withdrawals made, as described, the account would have a *balance* of $156.48 at the end of the year—a nice bonus!

By using this method, you would have earned an extra $156.48! See the chart in Figure 1.

Month	Pay	Income	Savings	Interest	Total Savings
September	$2,345.67	$1,563.78	$781.89	$0.00	$781.89
October	$2,345.67	$1,563.78	$1,563.78	$6.52	$1,570.30
November	$2,345.67	$1,563.78	$2,352.19	$9.80	$2,361.99
December	$2,345.67	$1,563.78	$3,143.88	$13.10	$3,156.98
January	$2,345.67	$1,563.78	$3,938.87	$16.41	$3,955.28
February	$2,345.67	$1,563.78	$4,737.17	$19.74	$4,756.91
March	$2,345.67	$1,563.78	$5,538.80	$23.08	$5,561.87
April	$2,345.67	$1,563.78	$6,343.76	$26.43	$6,370.20
May	$0.00	$1,563.78	$4,806.42	$20.03	$4,826.44
June	$0.00	$1,563.78	$3,262.66	$13.59	$3,276.26
July	$0.00	$1,563.78	$1,712.48	$7.14	$1,719.61
August	$0.00	$1,563.78	$155.83	$0.65	$156.48

Figure 1: An Example of How to Use a Savings Account to Normalize Irregular Incomes

Some employers offer to do all this work for their seasonal employees, that is, withhold a sum from each "real" paycheck so paydays continue throughout the year. But unless your employer is paying you interest, *they* are making extra money off of your hard-earned dollars! If you have the discipline not to touch your savings until the proper time, you are better off doing it yourself.

Other Options to Normalize your Income Events

While the use of a savings account is an easy and effective way to normalize Income Events, there are other techniques. In fact, the BudgetYes system itself can do the normalization within your checking account, and no separate savings account is needed. It does this by creating a sub-account within your checking account, and using that sub-account to accumulate money between Income Events. But, we are getting ahead of ourselves. If you are in the situation where you need to normalize your Income Events, know for now that you have several options. As you progress through this book and learn more about this budgeting system, you will be able to decide which method is right for you. Normalization using BudgetYes is discussed in Chapter 15, after a few more concepts have been defined in coming chapters.

The Difference Between Income and Bonuses

An important distinction must be made between your normal income and "bonuses"—unexpected and unplanned sums of money you may receive from time to time. For the purposes of planning Income Events, you should only consider the income you normally expect to receive. BudgetYes will take care of the bonuses automatically. If your sweet Aunt Marge always sends you a check for $50 on your birthday, do not worry about that when planning your budget. If you full well expect to receive a tax refund this year, just ignore it when defining your Income Events. As you will see, your new budgeting system will make sure that you get to spend your "bonus" money the way *you* want to spend it, rather than needing to use it for bills.

We do not mean to confuse bonuses with highly irregular incomes. Certainly, many individuals receive a large portion of the money they need to live on in the form of lump sum checks at the end of certain periods, or as commissions at times that are not completely predictable, or as a result of seasonal sales. These types of incomes need to be "smoothed out," or normalized, to distribute them throughout the year. By "bonuses," in this context, we mean truly unexpected windfalls that you do not depend on. The general guideline is to eliminate as many bonuses from your Income Events as possible.

Summary

The first step to setting up your budget is to resolve the difference between the frequency of your pay days, with the number of times you'll "enter" money into your budget. Most of the time an Income Event will be the same as your payday, but for those who have irregular incomes, they need to normalize the number of times money is entered into their budget to between one and four times a month.

 TIP: As a suggestion, if you are just getting into the habit of budgeting, start off with budgeting on a monthly basis (normalizing your income to once a month). Once you get that running smoothly, and maybe want to fine tune even more, then move to two or four times per month. The later examples in this book use a budget that runs on receiving income two times per month, but there is no reason you can't use a monthly budget.

Now that we have defined Income Events, let's take a look at the heart of the BudgetYes system: the Master Budget Sheet.

5

The Heart of BudgetYes

The Master Budget Sheet is the center around which the rest of the BudgetYes system revolves. It is the link between your income and what you want to do with that income—it allocates money from your Income Events for the budgeted items of your choosing.

> The *Master Budget Sheet* is the map that shows you when your money comes in, and where it goes. This is the cornerstone of the BudgetYes system.

This chapter will introduce you to the Master Budget Sheet, familiarize you with its basic parts, and give a quick overview of its workings. Later chapters will provide further explanations and plenty of examples.

Like much of the BudgetYes system, there is no single, authoritative format for the Master Budget Sheet. You can customize it to fit your needs. This book uses a generic format to explain the concepts, and an example of this format is presented in Figure 2. If you like this format and want to use it, a blank Master Budget Sheet for you to photocopy is provided in Appendix A. But after learning the basics, you might have other ideas for your personal Master Budget Sheets. In this case, you can grab a pencil, ruler, and some graph paper, and make up your own.

			Dates of Income Events						
Budget Item	Amount		8 4	9 1	10 13				
Grocery	475	00	✓	✓	✓				
Car Payment	276	12	420	430	441				
General Savings	100	00	8/15	9/15					
Gasoline	90	00	426	436					
Electric	65	00	8/22	9/22					
Natural Gas	45	00	423	433	444				
Exercise Class	25	00	428	438					
Total	1076	12							

Figure 2: An Example of a Master Budget Sheet

The Master Budget Sheet

The Master Budget Sheet is a chart that maps your Income Events to items you wish to budget for. The budget items are listed down the left side of the sheet, one per line, along with the amount budgeted for each item. In the example, the budget items are Grocery, for $475.00; Car Payment, for $276.12; General Savings, for $100.00; Gasoline, for $90.00; Electric (bill for home electricity), for $65.00; Natural Gas (home heating bill), for $45.00; and an Exercise Class for $25.00.

Right about now some very good questions are probably popping into your head. "Wait! How do I know how much to budget for each item? I don't spend the exact same amount at the grocery store every month, or for gasoline. How can I enter an amount for these?" These are all good and reasonable questions, and we promise that they will all be answered shortly. There are entire chapters dedicated to those answers. But for now, let's just become familiar with the Master Budget Sheet, and then address those important details later.

The last filled-in row of the sheet is a total line, which is simply the sum of all the budgeted amounts above it. This figure shows you the total amount you have budgeted for each Income Event.

Income Events Reserve Budgeted Amounts

Across the top of the sheet is a row of boxes labeled "Dates of Income Events." Every time an Income Event occurs, you should enter its date into the next open box. In Figure 2, three Income Events have been entered: August 4th, September 1st, and October 13th.

The key to the working of the Master Budget Sheet is that when an Income Event is recorded, it "reserves" all the budgeted amounts underneath it. When a "Dates of Income Events" box is filled in, all of the boxes beneath it become "activated", and reserve the amounts to which they correspond.

Looking again at the example, when the date of August 4th was filled in at the top of the column, that action automatically reserved $475.00 for groceries, $276.12 for a car payment, $100.00 for general savings, and so on right down the column.

Spending Budgeted Money

When it comes time to spend some of the money you have "reserved" using the Master Budget Sheet, record the transaction by marking the appropriate box. So when you spend money that came into your budget on August 4th for groceries, the box at the intersection of the "8/4" date and the Grocery budget item would be marked.

How to Mark Boxes

There are several ways the boxes can be marked. The easiest and most straightforward method is to use a check mark. You can see check marks in the example next to the Grocery budget item.

Another way to mark a box, that requires only a little additional effort but which has marvelous benefits, is to use the number of the check with which you paid for the transaction. In the example, this is the primary method used. You can see check number 420 was used for August's car payment, number 426 was used to pay the bill from the gasoline company, and number 433 was used for September's natural gas home heating payment.

$$\boxed{420}$$

The beauty of using check numbers is that, over time, an automatic cross-index into your checkbook is created. If you want to quickly find a particular check, or find all checks that were written for a particular purpose, it is easy. "What check did I use for my car payment in September?" A glance at the Master Budget Sheet shows you it was #430. "What were my natural gas payments for the last three months?" The "Natural Gas" row shows that you used checks #423, #433, and #444 for those payments. Pulling those checks, or looking up those numbers in your checkbook register, gives your answer.

Still another way to mark boxes is to use dates. Dates are useful when a check is not used for a transaction. In particular, automatic payments—bills that are paid through automatic deductions from your account via computer—can be recorded via dates. In the example, the General Savings and Electric items have been marked using dates.

$$\boxed{9/22}$$

Arrows can be used to mark several boxes at once. As you will see in later chapters, the Master Budget Sheet can save funds for large purchases that may occur several months in the future. When the time comes and you are ready to spend the money, an arrow can be used as a shortcut to mark several boxes at once, kind of a budgeting "tick-tack-toe."

In short, you can use any marking, symbol, or glyph that you like to record your transactions. Pick your favorites, experiment, and design techniques that you are the most comfortable with.

How many Master Budget Sheets?

You should set up Master Budget Sheets to correspond to the number of Income Events you have every month. So, for example, if you have two Income Events per month, you will need to complete two Master Budget Sheets. Each sheet will show how the corresponding portion of the month's income is budgeted.

Summary

The Master Budget Sheet is the centerpiece to the BudgetYes system. It is the guide to viewing your cash flow—when your money comes in, and how it leaves. The Master Budget Sheet is where you'll see the fruits of your labors, and become inspired and motivated to keep on improving your personal budget!

6

Your Spending Money

Working hand in hand with the Master Budget Sheet at the heart of the BudgetYes system is the "$" Account. Without doubt, this will be your favorite account, because it represents *your* money! The "$" Account contains the money you can spend on the things you want—it is the repository for the funds that are not budgeted.

> The "*$*" *Account* collects your spending money,
> the funds left over after all the bills are paid.

The "$" Account is a Virtual Account

Before we go any further, it is important to emphasize that the "$" Account isn't a "real" bank account or savings account. It is a tool you use to gain insights and understanding into how much spending money you have. The "$" Account exists within your checking account, and represents a specific subset of your total checking account balance. This is another implementation of the "overlay" concept described in Chapter 2. Exactly how the overlay works should become clear as we work through examples in upcoming chapters.

Your Refunds, Gifts, and Bonuses Go Here!

The "$" Account automatically accumulates extra money for you. If a bill comes whose payment amount is less than what you budgeted for, the leftover sum shows up in the "$" Account—and is then yours to spend. Similarly, if you receive a monetary gift, a bonus, a refund, or any other income outside of an Income Event, the "$" Account will collect it for you.

The "$" Account is also a Buffer

By the same token, this account automatically acts as a shock absorber and controlling vehicle for your entire BudgetYes system. If a bill arrives that is over the amount budgeted for it, the "$" Account can be used to cover the difference. Unexpected expenses, minor emergencies, or other unbudgeted expenditures can also be handled by these funds. True emergency funds should be established outside of the "$" Account (the typical guideline is to have three to six months of income saved), as discussed later in this book. Small emergencies, however, can be effectively handled by your "$" Account.

Like the Master Budget Sheet, there is no single, "correct" format that you have to use for your "$" Account. A standard format is used throughout this book, and is presented in Figure 3.

Date	Description	Amount		Balance	
				408	55
8/4	Payroll	+60	03	468	58
8/5	#419 Ozzie's Office Supplies	−14	30	454	28
8/10	#421 Telephone, pre-budget	−38	28	416	00
7/22	Watt Power, pre-budget	−18	16	397	84
8/1	Interest	+5	38	403	22
8/14	—Reconciled—				
8/18	Payroll	+168	90	572	12
8/22	#425 Bank Card	−307	18	264	94
8/22	#426 Gas Refund!	+16	78	281	72
9/1	Payroll	+60	03	341	75
9/9	#431 Telephone Refund!	+4	75	346	50
9/9	Aunt Marge's Gift	+50	00	396	50
8/22	Electric—Over Budget	−12	12	384	38
9/1	Interest	+2	46	386	84
9/5	Printed Check Fee	−4	50	382	34
9/11	—Reconciled—				
9/15	Payroll	+168	90	551	24
9/16	#434 Bank Card	−128	68	422	56
9/23	#436 Gasoline Refund!	+7	30	429	86
9/29	Payroll—Triple!!!	+1136	15	1566	01
9/30	#439 Stereo	−505	41	1060	60
10/9	Transfer (Natural Gas)	−50	00	1010	60
10/13	Payroll	+60	03	1070	63
10/13	#442 Telephone Refund!	+10	02	1080	65
10/13	#443 Halloween Show	−26	50	1054	15
9/22	Electric Refund!	+2	72	1056	87
10/1	Interest	+3	37	1060	24
10/13	—Reconciled—				
10/18	#445 Bank Card	−360	12	700	12

Figure 3: An Example of a "$" Account

In the example, the first (left-most) column is for the date of the transaction—the date that money either enters or leaves the account.

The second column is for a description of each transaction. You can write anything you like here: notes, summaries, memos—the same kind of reminders you might use in your checkbook, or on the "memo" line of your checks, to help you remember the nature of the transaction. One very helpful practice is to include the number of the check corresponding to the entry, if applicable. So, for example, if check #431 gave you a "refund" because, luckily, the amount you needed to pay was less than what you had budgeted, you could place the number "431" in the description column as a cross-reference to the check in question. There will be plenty of examples of these kinds of entries in upcoming chapters.

Some people only enter dates and check numbers in the description column—without any other explanatory text—as a kind of quick shorthand, knowing they could look up details in their checkbook if necessary. Pick whatever method works best for you.

The third column in the example is for the amount of the transaction. This is the amount that is either being added to or deducted from the "$" Account total.

The final (right-most) column of the ledger is for computation of the balance, or running total, of the "$" Account. Just like your checkbook total, the last completed line in this column shows the current amount of money in your "$" Account. Again, this is *your* money! If you've set everything up correctly, then all your other expenses have guaranteed reserved funds set aside. Money is saved in your checking account for the telephone bill, the car payment, the groceries. The "$" Account is for what *you* want!

You probably recognize the layout of the example as the familiar ledger format used in your checkbook register. So, you have lots of options for creating the "$" Account format you will use. If you like the format used within this book, a blank sample is available in Appendix B for photocopying. If you have empty, unused checkbook ledgers available, you may use one of those, or photocopy some blank pages from your current checkbook. Alternatively, office supply stores carry dozens of different accounting ledger books—pick out one you like, or browse them for ideas. And again, you can get creative with a pencil, ruler, and some graph paper, and design your own custom format.

A Budget Snapshot—For You and Others

Because of the way the BudgetYes system is set up and operates, the "$" Account is an excellent quick summary of the state of your budget, for either yourself, a family member, or a significant other. Want to know how your budget is doing? Just glance at the last line of your "$" Account.

Sometimes, in households, one person takes charge of running the budget and paying the bills. But, naturally, a spouse or other interested party may need to know the state of the household budget. Rather than that other person needing to review the entire budget system and checkbook entries, they can just look at the "$" Account for a snapshot summary.

Summary

The "$" Account is very simple, yet extremely powerful. It tells you what you really need to know: how much "extra" money you have—money above and beyond the normal monthly expenses.

7

Types of Budget Items

Let's look now in more detail at the types of items you can budget for using the BudgetYes system. Although the basic idea behind budgeting for any expenditure is always the same—saving money *up front* for expenses that you know are coming later—different item types exist to deal with the variability in payments that you will encounter. Some expenses such as your car payment, rent, or house payment, may be for the same amount every month. Other bills, such as heating, electricity, or other utilities, may vary widely on a monthly basis. Categorization of each expense into the proper type will allow you to apply the appropriate accounting techniques and tricks to smooth out the peaks and valleys, avoid surprises, and make the most of your hard-earned money.

The BudgetYes system is comprised of three types of budget items: Simple Budget Items, Bounded Budget Items, and Monitored Budget Items. Each of these three types will now be examined in detail.

Simple Budget Items

The easiest type of item to budget for is an expense or payment that is the same every month. You always know the exact amount you'll need to pay, and you usually know the exact date the payment will be due. Because these types of items make budgeting so easy for you, they are called *Simple Budget Items*.

> A *Simple Budget Item* is an expense that is the same every month. Typical examples are house and car payments.

Entering an amount for a Simple Budget Item into your Master Budget Sheet is, well, simple. ☺ The amount you enter is the amount of your monthly expense.

There are lots of examples of Simple Budget Items on the sample Master Budget Sheet we examined earlier. Let's take another look; the sheet is presented again in Figure 4.

Dates of
Income Events

Budget Item	Amount		8 4	9 1	10 13				
Grocery	475	00	✓	✓	✓				
Car Payment	276	12	420	430	441				
General Savings	100	00	8/15	9/15					
Gasoline	90	00	426	436					
Electric	65	00	8/22	9/22					
Natural Gas	45	00	423	433	444				
Exercise Class	25	00	428	438					
Total	1076	12							

Figure 4: A Master Budget Sheet Containing Some Simple Budget Items.

Here, the second budget item, the Car Payment, is a Simple Budget Item. The payment is the same every month—it is always $276.12, and hence qualifies. The next item, General Savings, is a "self-imposed" Simple Budget Item. Here, the person is making a commitment to put $100.00 every pay into a savings account. Finally, the last item on the sheet, the Exercise Class, is also a Simple Budget Item.

Simple Budget Items can also cover items that have just one or two payments per year, automatically saving money for you until the bill comes. A classic example of this is car insurance, which typically requires a premium payment either semi-annually or annually. Suppose, for example, that your car insurance payment was $253.50 every six months. Rather than being hit with this relatively large bill every half year, you can save a little every month, guaranteeing that the full payment will be available to you when you need it.[3] For a semiannual payment of $253.50, you need to save $42.25 every month. This type of Simple Budget Item is shown on a different sample of a Master Budget Sheet, presented in Figure 5. By the way, there are three other Simple Budget Items on this second example. The House Payment is always $755.00 every month. The General Savings item is the same as the one on the first sheet, except it reserves $100.00 from the second pay of the month. And the Donations item is another self-imposed Simple Budget Item—here, the person is making a commitment to donate $20.00 every month to a worthwhile cause.

---

[3] An additional benefit of this technique is that you will earn interest on the money while it is being saved, hence end up with some nice additions to your "$" Account! You also avoid "partial payment" fees. These semi-annual bills may charge extra if you choose to pay quarterly or monthly.

Budget Item	Amount		Dates of Income Events							
			8 18	9 15						
House Payment	755	00	424	435						
General Savings	100	00	8/30	9/30						
Telephone	50	00	431	442						
Car Insurance	42	25								
Donations	20	00	446	→						
Total	967	25								

Figure 5: A Different Master Budget Sheet Showing Further Examples of Simple Budget Items

TIP: It is important to use exact amounts when budgeting, rather than rounding. For a car payment of $276.12, it might be tempting not to worry about the twelve cents. But keeping track of everything right down to the penny will actually save you work in the long run. A process called *Reconciling*, explained in Chapter 13, can be used to check for errors, and ensure your budget and your checkbook are still in perfect synch. Reconciling depends on the pennies for the internal consistency checks; without them, you would be forced to do additional work to account for the discrepancies.

One final clarification might help define Simple Budget Items. Suppose it is October, and the exercise class fee is $25.00. But coming up at the first of the year, you know there is going to be an increase. So for the next six months, your exercise class fee is not going to be the same every time. Is it still a Simple Budget Item? The answer is yes. As long as a payment is usually the same for some period of time, it should probably be considered a simple budget item. Changes to the budget amount (such as an annual fee increase) are handled via Changes to Your Budget, described in Chapter 14.

Bounded Budget Items

Unfortunately, not all budget items afford you the simplicity of having the same payment amount month in and month out. The next level of complexity involves those payments that are more or less the same every month, but still have a maximum cap. Because these payments bounce around within certain well-understood bounds, they are called *Bounded Budget Items*.

> A *Bounded Budget Item* is an expense that is more or less the same every month, but has a maximum cap. Examples are telephone bills and water bills.

The key to budgeting Bounded Budget Items is to pick amounts that will cover most normal bills without tying up too much money. To do this, you must recognize exception cases and eliminate artificial maximums.

Picking the Amount for the Bounded Item

The best way to decide on an amount for a Bounded Budget Item is to examine the bills from the last year or two. Pick a value that will cover most of the bills without tying up excessive amounts of money.

As an example of selecting a prudent amount, suppose your telephone bills for the last year were as follows:

Month	Phone Bill	Month	Phone Bill
January:	$43.16	July:	$49.00
February:	$47.50	August:	$42.07
March:	$99.15	September:	$38.24
April:	$52.98	October:	$22.10
May:	$39.42	November:	$45.57
June:	$44.33	December:	$50.61

Looking over these amounts, one bill is conspicuously out of line with all the others: the March bill for $99.15. This bill is about double any other amount on the list! Chances are good that with a bill this large, something out of the ordinary occurred and there will be an explanation for the anomaly. Perhaps you became engaged to be married that month and called all of your friends and relatives to share the good news. Perhaps you bought a house, and had to make a lot of telephone calls to close on it. Whatever the reason, this unusual bill should be ignored for your planning purposes. If you were to budget for it, you would be setting aside a large amount of money to cover an unlikely circumstance.

Ignoring the exception case of the March bill then, most of the other bills seem to fall somewhere between forty and fifty dollars. Yes, there are a couple that are over fifty dollars, but not by much. And there are three that are under forty dollars. Two of those lower bills are very close to forty dollars, and the third (October for $22.10) is so low that it can fairly be considered to be another exception case.

Armed with this knowledge, you are now in a position to choose an amount. Certainly, one sensible value would be $50.00. This would cover the majority of the bills. Alternatively, you might pick $55.00, to give yourself a little breathing room.

Another option might arise if you wanted to challenge yourself to aggressively lower your average monthly telephone bill. By picking an amount such as $45.00 or even $40.00, you could give yourself an incentive or target to shoot for.

All of these choices are yours. Remember—you are building *your* budget. Make it work for you to accomplish the goals you have in mind!

No History of Past Bills?

It might be, for any number of reasons, that you do not have a history of past bills to examine for trends. Maybe you just moved to a larger home in a new neighborhood, and don't know what your typical bills will be. The best advice is to ask around. Very often, utility companies will gladly furnish typical usage patterns and average bill amounts. Your friends and neighbors can also be tapped for estimates and recommendations. For apartments, landlords can usually furnish accurate data. If you have just purchased a previously-owned home, consider asking the prior owner for ideas.

Working With Your Chosen Amount

Suppose you choose $50.00 for your telephone budget amount, and a bill comes for $52.98, as it did in the April example of last year. Where does the extra $2.98 come from? The "$" Account. Here is a concrete example of that account acting as a shock absorber to smooth out a slight variation in your budget plans.

The use of the "$" Account might also shed some light as to why $50.00 might be a good amount to choose for the telephone budget. Ignoring the exception case of March of last year, the eleven other months would have been covered nicely by only withdrawing $3.59 from your "$" Account—$2.98 in April and 61 cents in December.

Conversely, what happens when a bill comes in *under* the $50.00 amount? That's right—the extra money goes *into* your "$" Account! So, for example, had your budget been in place last October when you received that low bill of $22.10, your "$" Account would have received a nice bonus of $27.90—all for you to spend!

✓ NOTE: Judicious selection of your Bounded Budget Item amounts, working hand in hand with your "$" Account, can lead to you receiving "refunds" every time you sit down to pay bills. Now there's a switch—after a morning of writing checks, you might have more money to spend than when you started!

Monitored Budget Items

We have now covered two types of expenses: those that are exactly the same every month, and those that are generally within certain bounds. The last type to study involves that collection of bills that vary widely from month to month. Heating bills, for example, might be minuscule in the summer, and budget busters during the winter. Grocery bills often become unwieldy during holiday periods, when you might find yourself with a houseful of friends and relatives to feed.

The trick the BudgetYes system uses to tame these widely fluctuating demands on your money is to set up a separate, internal account—much like the "$" Account—to monitor the expense.

Because of the monitoring abilities that the separate accounts provide for you, these types of budget items are called *Monitored Budget Items*.

> A *Monitored Budget Item* is an expense that varies widely every month, or one that you need or want to monitor. Examples might be grocery expenses, heating bills, and electric bills.

Just like Simple Budget Items and Bounded Budget Items, the amount you budget for a Monitored Budget Item is the same every month. This gives you the control and predictability you need. But different things will happen when you pay your bill, depending on the circumstance.

To show how this all works, let's return for a moment to the example of your home heating bill. Just for now, let's pretend you use natural gas for home heating, and your monthly budgeted amount for that expense is $45.00. (Naturally, we'll be discussing how to arrive at good budget amounts in just a moment.) Let's also pretend it is a warm June, and the only thing you are using natural gas for is your hot water. It would not be surprising to receive a bill that was way under budget; let's say it was for $16.14.

If your natural gas budget item was a Bounded Budget Item, you would pay the $16.14 and put the remaining $28.86 ($45.00 minus $16.14) into your "$" Account. But with a Monitored Budget Item, that extra $28.86 gets "transferred" to a special *Monitored Budget Account*, where it is saved until needed. If you use this same technique all through the hot summer, then just like a squirrel storing nuts for the winter, your Monitored Budget Account will accumulate funds for those high heating bills during the cold months of the year. Suppose it's January, and you receive a bill for $92.50. Forty-five dollars of that amount will come from your normal monthly budgeted amount. The remaining $47.50 would be "withdrawn" from the Monitored Budget Account.

> A *Monitored Budget Account* is just like the "$"
> Account Sheet you learned about in Chapter 6.
> Instead of monitoring your spending money, a
> Monitored Budget Account can be set up for any
> Monitored Budget Item (expense), you choose.

If you have realized the money that accumulates in a Monitored Budget Account is working hard and earning interest for you, you're probably smiling.

As mentioned in the definition above, one piece of good news is that you are already familiar with the format of a Monitored Budget Account—it is identical to whatever ledger format you pick for your "$" Account. As a matter of fact, the "$" Account *is* a Monitored Budget Account—just a very special one. All Monitored Budget Accounts are simply records detailing how money flows in and out of the account.

Figure 6 presents an example of a Monitored Budget Account. This one happens to be monitoring grocery expenses.

Date	Description	Amount		Balance	
8/4	Payroll	+475	00	475	00
8/12	#422 Phude Groceries, Inc.	–128	64	346	36
8/14	—Reconcile—				
8/27	#427 Phude Groceries, Inc.	–198	96	147	40
9/1	Payroll	+475	00	622	40
9/4	#429 Phude Groceries, Inc.	–246	87	375	53
9/12	#432 Phude Groceries, Inc.	–82	34	293	19
9/11	—Reconcile—				
9/23	#437 Phude Groceries, Inc.	–163	27	129	92
10/7	#440 Phude Groceries, Inc.	–78	05	51	87
10/13	Payroll	+475	00	526	87
10/13	—Reconcile—				

Figure 6: An Example of a Monitored Budget Account

Every item you choose to monitor will need to have a separate Monitored Budget Account set up. This simply involves creating one ledger sheet for each item by writing its name at the top: Grocery, Home Heating, Electric, or whatever your choices are.

✓ NOTE: It is probably worth reinforcing at this point all of these "accounts" are not actual separate bank accounts. The Monitored Budget Accounts are virtual accounts that exist *within* your checking account. Each of these subdivisions hold and reserve money for the expense to which they're dedicated, and impart control and understanding to how your checking account dollars and cents are allocated.

 TIP: The sum of all the monies in your Monitored Budget Accounts, your "$" Account, and the amounts you have reserved in your Master Budget Sheets will total your current checkbook balance.

Picking the Amount for the Monitored Item

How do you decide on the amount to budget for a Monitored Budget Item? One way that works very well is to use the average of your payments for the last year or two. Thus, add up all the payments for the last year and divide that sum by 12, or add up all the payments for the last two years and divide that sum by 24. The resulting answer should perform very well for you as a budget amount; you may be pleasantly surprised at how well such a simple forecasting method will perform in budgeting your needs throughout the year.

There is another way you can arrive at the amount to budget for certain Monitored Budget Items. This one involves having a team of professional forecasters analyze usage trends, study climatological data for your area, and use sophisticated computer algorithms to come up with a very accurate amount especially for your budget—all for *free*.

Interested? Many utility companies offer budgeting plans for their customers. With names like the "Easy Budget Plan" or the "Smart Payment Plan", services are offered that allow you to pay the same amount every month, smoothing out your payments for the entire year. (Is this beginning to sound familiar?) The utilities always start these plans during the low usage periods, thus allowing their customers to build up "credit" or a reserve of funds when bills are low. This buildup of money is then used to satisfy the demands of big bills later in the year.

What do you suppose the utility companies do with the extra money they receive when the budget plans are getting started? Sure—the money is invested, earning interest and dividends for the company. In fact, for many utility companies, such budget plans are major profit centers, producing millions of dollars of additional income.

Please don't misunderstand: none of this is meant as criticism of the utilities. They are businesses, and the budget plans help them collect money that is due and keep their costs low. The plans also provide a valuable public service by making it possible for many customers to pay who ordinarily could not. But the point is, why give extra money to a utility company so they can invest it, when you could be earning interest from your hard-earned dollars yourself?

Most people who want to budget their utility bills have to use the utility company plans because they have no way of implementing such a "pay-ahead" scheme themselves. But with the BudgetYes system's Monitored Budget Account, you have a way.

Let's return to determining the amount to budget for your utility Monitored Budget Items. As was alluded to earlier, the utility companies have specialized teams of professional forecasters and computer systems to determine very accurate budget amounts for their "E-Z Payment Plans." Often, these amounts are printed on your utility bill as an incentive to joining the plan. ("If you want to join our E-Z Payment Plan, your monthly budget amount would be such-and-so.") Well, you can use that budget amount for your Monitored Budget Item, and reap all the benefits of the research and planning of an entire department of skilled forecasters!

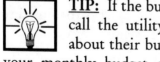 **TIP:** If the budget amount is not printed on your bill, call the utility company, tell them you are curious about their budget plan and would like to know what your monthly budget amount would be. When you get the number, thank them, tell them you're not interested, and then put the number on your Master Budget Sheet. The utility com-

pany will benefit, because they will have a customer who faithfully pays all their bills on time. You will benefit by having an accurate budget amount with little work on your part, by earning extra interest, and by establishing a good paying history with the utility.

Like the Simple Budget Items that were discussed earlier, you can play with the budget amounts you choose for your Monitored Budget Items. You can add a little as a cushion, or list an amount to shoot for, as a way of reducing your overall expenses.

Occasionally, you will need to "settle up" your Monitored Budget Items. At the end of the year, or the end of the cold heating season, for example, it might be your Monitored Budget Account for home heating is empty, and you've been drawing heavily on the "$" Account to make up the difference. In this case, you'll need to increase the monthly budget amount for the item for the coming year. On the other hand, you might have a surplus saved in a Monitored Budget Account you didn't need to use. This nice bonus can be transferred over to your "$" Account. Techniques for these kinds of budget adjustments will be covered in Chapters 14 and 15.

Summary

A Simple Budget Item is an expense that is the same every month. A Bounded Budget Item is more or less the same, with a maximum cap. A Monitored Budget Item varies widely every month.

8

Putting It All Together

We have now covered enough of the basic BudgetYes components to combine them into a completely functional budgeting system. To illustrate how all the parts work together, we will set up a budget for a hypothetical family and run it for them for several weeks.

Let us state from the outset that the *amounts* in this chapter—the payroll, bills, and budgeted items—are *not* important. It is quite likely that the illustrative amounts presented here will either be higher or lower than any corresponding items in your particular situation. What you need to learn from this chapter is the *mechanics* and *functioning* of the BudgetYes system: how it works.

Please do not come to the conclusion that because the budget of the hypothetical family presented here is different than your own, that the BudgetYes system will not work for you. It will. Just think of these as arbitrary amounts used to demonstrate the accounting techniques.

Income and Deductions

Income. Let's pick a nice, round number for the family's annual income—say about $50,000 per year. We'll also say that the paydays occur every two weeks, on Fridays, so the family has two Income Events per month.[4]

✓ **NOTE:** The first budgeting item we will discuss is an important one: retirement savings. Assume that the employer has a pre-tax retirement savings plan. These plans allow money for retirement investments to be automatically deducted from your pay, and because of special laws, you do not have to pay any taxes on the money so deducted. Hence, the pre-tax retirement savings plans have the double benefit of helping with your future security and reducing your tax liability.

Deductions. In our example, let's assume that the family has committed to saving $150 per pay, or $300 per month, in a pre-tax plan. Because this money is deducted before the family ever "sees" it, it is not something that needs to be listed in the budget sheets.

In fact, any deduction that is made from your pay, be it state, local, or federal taxes; savings; health and dental plans; Social

---

[4] Because of the uneven distribution of weeks and months within the calendar, if you're paid every other week, there will be two or three months wherein there will be three paydays instead of two. This phenomenon, known as "The Magnificent Triple", will be covered in a later chapter. For now, just plan the budget on two Income Events per month.

Security and Medicare; or whatever, should not be entered into your BudgetYes system. *Your personal budget is a plan for how to spend the money you actually get to take home.*

✓ **NOTE:** If you are self-employed, run a small business, work under contract, are paid on a per-job basis, or have any type of income where an employer does not automatically make deductions for you, then you *should* consider budgeting for items such as taxes, health insurance, and the like.

Our example payroll amount does have an employer making deductions, including the $150 per pay that the family has committed to for retirement savings. After all deductions, let's say that the family's take-home pay is $1,136.15, every other week.

Picking Budget Items and Amounts

With those basics out of the way, it's now time for the family to decide on the items to budget for, and the amount to budget for each item. To do this, they will use all the techniques presented in the previous chapters: examining the list of items presented in Appendix C, consulting histories of past bills and usage trends, looking at the bills they pay frequently, and deciding where they would like to cut back and aggressively challenge themselves to save.

Let's say that the family has talked together, done their homework, and come up with the following items and amounts to budget for every month:

Monthly Expenses	
House Payment	$755.00
Grocery	$475.00
Car Payment	$276.12
General Savings	$200.00
Gasoline	$90.00
Electric	$65.00
Telephone	$50.00
Natural Gas	$45.00
Car Insurance	$42.25
Exercise Class	$25.00
Donations	$20.00

Setting up the Budget

We now have a list of the items to budget for, an amount associated with each item, and we know there are two Income Events per month. The next step is to distribute the budgeted items between the two Income Events.

When are the bills due? Most of the time, the decision of which part of the month to budget an item for will be obvious or easy to determine based on when the payment is due. Let's look at a few facts about the example family's payments and due dates, and then see how they could be budgeted for.

✓ The house payment is due on the 1st of every month.

✓ When setting up their new budget, the family made an increased commitment to general savings, that is, saving for emergencies or opportunities. They have made arrangements with their bank to automatically transfer $100 from the checking account to the savings account twice a month—once on the 15th, and again on the 30th.

✓ The car payment is due on the 20th.

✓ The telephone bill is due early in the month.

✓ The electric company that serves the family's home allows payments by automatic computer transfers from a checking account. This automatic payment plan eliminates the need to write a check, pay postage, or worry about making payments in time. The family has signed up for this plan; the automatic deduction occurs on the 22nd of each month.

✓ The gasoline and natural gas (home heating) bills are due late in the month.

✓ The fee for the exercise class needs to be paid near the end of every month.

With these facts in hand, we can now begin to distribute the various items to the two Income Events. The general rule to use is to budget early enough in the month to make sure that the money is there when you need it, but not so early that the money will sit idly for long periods. If there are two Income Events every month, this generally translates into budgeting for an item in the opposite half of a month from when it is due. Another way of stating this is to allocate funds for a payment approximately two weeks before its due date.

Let's look at the family's house payment, for example, due on the 1st of every month. Since this bill has to be paid early in the month, the family should budget it for their second Income Event.

This might be worth some further explanation. If paydays come every other Friday, the first pay of the month could arrive anywhere between the 1st and the 14th, depending on the pay cycle and how the month's calendar happens to fall. If the house payment were to be budgeted for the first Income Event (the first pay of the month), the family would be in a crunch to make the payment, due on the 1st, if the money didn't arrive until nearly two weeks later! What about budgeting the house payment for the first Income Event, and then using that saved amount for the *following* month's payment? That would tie up the $755 for weeks, hurting the family's cash flow.

Hence, using the facts presented above about due dates, we can now distribute the family's budget items across the two Income Events. The House Payment and Telephone items are both due early in the month, so they are allocated to the Income Event for the second part of the month. The Car Payment, Gasoline, Electric, Natural Gas, and Exercise Class items are all due late in the month, so they are allocated to the first Income Event. The $100 deduction for the General Savings item occurs twice a month, so both Income Events get an entry for that.

Expenses with no exact due date. Many budget items will have no fixed due dates, such as the Grocery and Donations items in our example. Other items will be saving up for expenses far in the future, such as the Car Insurance item, vacations, new vehicles, or furniture purchases. It does not matter which Income Event these types of items are allocated to. You can distribute them evenly, to try to make the total amounts of the budgeted items for both Income Events more or less the same, or sort them in any way that makes sense to you.

Splitting up an expense item. Budget items can be split up across Income Events, as well. For the example we've been following, there is no reason that the family has to allocate its entire allotment of $475 for groceries to the first Income Event. Alternatively, $250 could be allocated to the first part of the month, and $225 to the second.

 TIP: One final idea is that many banks, utilities, and other creditors will gladly change the due dates of bills. If this will better balance out your Income Event allocations, or make your budgeting easier, call and ask. Often, when a creditor learns that you are starting a new budget, they will know they will be able to rely on your future payments and will be more than happy to accommodate your request.

Presented below is the distribution of the hypothetical family's budgeted items across their two Income Events, along with totals.

First Part of the Month		Second Part of the Month	
Grocery	$475.00	House Payment	$755.00
Car Payment	$276.12	General Savings	$100.00
General Savings	$100.00	Telephone	$50.00
Gasoline	$90.00	Car Insurance	$42.25
Electric	$65.00	Donations	$20.00
Natural Gas	$45.00		
Exercise Class	$25.00		
Total	$1,076.12	Total	$967.25

BudgetYes Sheets for Sample Family Budget

We are now ready to make up the BudgetYes sheets for this family. The two Master Budget Sheets can be created directly from the above table, and are shown in Figure 7 and Figure 8.

Budget Item	Amount		Dates of Income Events							
Grocery (Monitored)	475	00								
Car Payment	276	12								
General Savings	100	00								
Gasoline	90	00								
Electric	65	00								
Natural Gas (Monitored)	45	00								
Exercise Class	25	00								
Total	1076	12								

Figure 7: The Newly-created Master Budget Sheet for the First Part of the Month

During their decision-making process about what to budget for, the family decided that the Grocery and Natural Gas items would be Monitored Budget Items. To complete the BudgetYes sheets, then, they would make up two Monitored Budget Accounts. Creating these accounts only involves writing the terms "Grocery" and "Natural Gas" at the top of two blank Monitored Budget Account sheets.

Budget Item	Amount		Dates of Income Events							
House Payment	755	00								
General Savings	100	00								
Telephone	50	00								
Car Insurance	42	25								
Donations	20	00								
Total	967	25								

Figure 8: The Newly-created Master Budget Sheet for the Second Part of the Month

Also, the family needs to create their "$" Account. This is done by taking another blank Monitored Budget Account sheet and placing a "$" at the top.

Starting the Budget

Finally, to initialize the BudgetYes system, the family should copy their current checkbook balance into the "$" Account. This is the action that "jump starts" the system and initializes the overlay process.

A natural question at this point is when good times are to start the BudgetYes system. In fact, the system is designed so it can begin at any time—you could initiate it immediately if you so desired. Alternatively, certain times offer inviting "clean breaks" and make excellent starting points: January 1st (or the beginning of any month), the beginning of a quarter or tax period, the first day of a new job, the day you move into a new home, or the day you return from your honeymoon.

 TIP: Aside from commencement dates such as those just cited, there is a situation to watch for that will minimize the amount of start-up work you needed to get the BudgetYes system up and running. The time to watch for is when you have most of your bills paid, and an Income Event is about to occur. As you will see shortly, the accounting tricks you are about to learn take about a month to completely catch up with your bill-paying habits. The more bills from the last month you can have taken care of before you start running your budget, the easier it will be, and the less special work you will have to do during the first month.

Summary

For our example budget, we chose the items to budget for, and the corresponding target amounts. We distributed the items between the two monthly Income Events by setting up two Master Budget Sheets. We also set up two Monitored Budget Account sheets, one for Grocery, one for Natural Gas. Finally, we initialized our "special" Monitored Budget Account sheet, the "$" Account, with the family's current checkbook balance, and we are ready to go. Turn the page to watch BudgetYes run!

9

Running BudgetYes

This chapter will show, in detail, the day-to-day running of the BudgetYes system for several weeks of a family's paydays, bills, and expenses. You may find it helpful to create the five new BudgetYes sheets, just described in the last section, and follow along as the scenario progresses.

To complete the picture, we need to look at one more item: the family checkbook. This is presented in Figure 9. It should be emphasized that Figure 9 is not another form you have to create or fill out. This is just a representation of the checkbook register you've been using all along.

DATE	NO.	TRANSACTION DESCRIPTION	✓	DEPOSIT	PAYMENT	BALANCE 509 95
7/30	417	Refined Oil Company			76 40	433 55
8/1	418	Jumpin' Pumpin' Aerobics			25 00	408 55
8/1		—Budget starts here—				408 55

Figure 9: A Checkbook Register

 TIP: Chapter 2 discussed the importance of using an interest bearing checking account. Most such accounts require a minimum balance, such as $1,000, to ensure that they will earn interest or not incur penalty fees. One technique for making sure you do not drop below that minimum balance is *not* to reflect the amount in your checkbook—so you won't be tempted to cross the line. This trick is used in Figure 9. The actual checking account balance is $1,408.55. However, the family has chosen not to include the $1,000 minimum amount, so $408.55 shows as the balance. Since the extra thousand doesn't appear in the register, there is a reduced temptation to dip into those funds. When the monthly checking account statement arrives from your financial institution, it is usually an easy matter to mentally add the $1,000 back in to make sure your checkbook balances with the statement.

 TIP: When you begin your budget, it is a good idea to mark the point where your budget starts. Draw a colored line across the page at that point, and/or write an indication on the next blank line that this is where your budget is beginning.

 NOTE: When you start your budget, your checkbook should be up to date, with all checks entered, all arithmetic done and verified, and in agreement with your latest bank statement. Remember, BudgetYes is an *overlay* of your checking account. It can only work as well as the account that it is overlaying.

As was already mentioned, you "prime the pump" for the BudgetYes system by copying your current checkbook balance into your "$" Account. For this example, the current checkbook balance is $408.55: the resulting new "$" Account is shown in Figure 10.

Date	Description	Amount	Balance	
			408	55

Figure 10: An Initialized "$" Account

The BudgetYes system is now ready to roll.

Example: Money Enters the Budget

It is Friday, August 4th, and it is a payday—the family's first Income Event under their new budget. This pay would be entered in the checkbook, as usual (see Figure 11). Now, just a few other tasks have to be done.

DATE	NO.	TRANSACTION DESCRIPTION	✓	DEPOSIT		PAYMENT		BALANCE 509	95
7/30	417	Refined Oil Company				76	40	433	55
8/1	418	Jumpin' Pumpin' Aerobics				25	00	408	55
8/1		—Budget starts here—						408	55
8/4		Payroll		1136	15			1544	70

Figure 11: August 4th Pay Entered into the Checkbook Register

Since an Income Event has occurred, the date must be entered into the appropriate Master Budget Sheet, in this case, the sheet for the first part of the month. This action is shown in Figure 12.

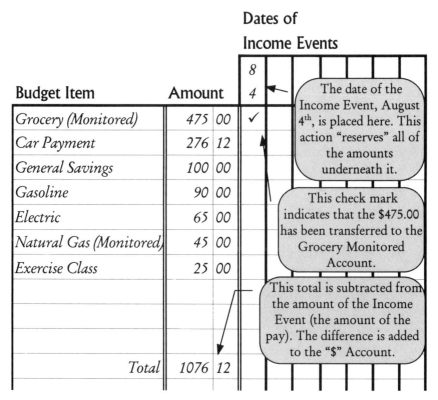

Figure 12: Updates to the Master Budget Sheet (First Part of the Month) for the August 4th Pay

The second step involves the total at the bottom of the Master Budget Sheet. The payroll amount is $1136.15, and the amount budgeted for that pay is $1076.12. The difference, $60.03, is unbudgeted money, and goes directly into the "$" Account. This addition is shown in Figure 13.

Date	Description	Amount		Balance	
				408	55
8/4	*Payroll*	+60	03	468	58

Figure 13: Update to the "$" Account for the August 4th Pay

We should mention here that it is common to only have a small addition to your "$" Account as a result of an Income Event, particularly when you are first starting your budget. Here, the family has allowed themselves about $60 for their account, but amounts of $10 or even less are not unusual. The secret is that if you have done a good job of budgeting and follow the incentive to stick to the spending limits you have established, then extra money will be "released" when you pay bills and will flow into the "$" Account as "refunds." You are in charge—the BudgetYes system acts as your instrument panel to let you know how you are doing.

One final action needs to be performed to process the August 4th Income Event. This action involves transferring money to the Grocery Monitored Budget Account, and warrants further explanation.

As you have seen, this family has created two Monitored Budget Accounts: one for Grocery and the other for Natural Gas. Though these are both Monitored Items, the bills are paid differently for each. For the Natural Gas item, there is only one bill per month. The Monitored Budget Account exists to "smooth out" the seasonal variations throughout the year. The Grocery item, on the other hand, will have many "withdrawals" made throughout the month as various runs to the market are made. The purpose here is to manage the month's Grocery allotment, moderating between major trips to stock up for meals and quick runs for snacks or forgotten items.

Because of the different nature of the two Monitored Items, the accounting methods used for each will be handled differently in these examples. Because the Grocery Monitored Budget Account will see a lot of activity, we will transfer the money there as soon as the Income Event occurs. For the Natural Gas item, on the other hand, we will only add or subtract money from the Monitored Budget Account when the bill is paid.

Transferring money from a Master Budget Sheet to a Monitored Budget Account is simple. If you glance back at Figure 12, you will see a check mark next to the Grocery item, indicating that the $475 has been moved over. Figure 14 shows the corresponding entry on the Grocery Monitored Account.

Date	Description	Amount		Balance	
8/4	Payroll	+475	00	475	00

Figure 14: The Initialization of the Grocery Monitored Account

We have now completed all the steps associated with an Income Event. Though we have spent several pages describing the procedures, rest assured that in actual practice this takes significantly less time to do than it does to explain!

> **Recap: Processing an Income Event**
>
> All we did was enter a date and a check mark on the Master Budget Sheet, perform a subtraction, and make two entries on separate Monitored Account sheets (one of which was the special "$" Account).

Example: Spending Unbudgeted Money

Let's say that the next day, inspired by their new budget, the family stops at the local office supply store for some new file folders, a few colored markers, an eraser or two, and some photocopies of the BudgetYes sheets. (By the way, new supplies can be a terrific incentive to commit to a new budgeting system, and can be concrete proof of your new mode of being organized. You might consider such a purchase for yourself to help launch your new budget.) Let's pretend the total comes to $14.30, and that the family pays by check. This entry to the checkbook register is shown in Figure 15.

								BALANCE	
DATE	NO.	TRANSACTION DESCRIPTION	✓	DEPOSIT		PAYMENT		509	95
7/30	417	Refined Oil Company				76	40	433	55
8/1	418	Jumpin' Pumpin' Aerobics				25	00	408	55
8/1		—Budget starts here—						408	55
8/4		Payroll		1136	15			1544	70
8/5	419	Ozzie's Office Supplies				14	30	1530	40

Figure 15: The Checking Account Entry for Check #419 for Office Supplies

This purchase was unbudgeted—there is nothing on either of the Master Budget Sheets for office supplies or file folders. This is a case where the family decided to spend some the funds in their "$" Account, and the $14.30 should be deducted from there. Figure 16 shows the amount deducted from the "$" Account, leaving a balance of $454.28.

Date	Description	Amount	Balance
			408 55
8/4	Payroll	+60 03	468 58
8/5	#419 Ozzie's Office Supplies	−14 30	454 28

Figure 16: The "$" Account Entry for Check #419 for Office Supplies

Recap: Writing a Check for an Expense *Not* Covered in Budget

An entry was made in the "$" Account.

Example: Simple Budget Item

The next day, the family puts the car payment in the mail. The entry in the checkbook is made as usual (see Figure 17). Since the car payment is a Simple Budget Item, the corresponding budget entry for it is easy. All that has to be done is to place the number of the check used for the payment within the proper box on the Master Budget Sheet. This entry is shown in Figure 18.

| | | | | | | | | BALANCE | |
DATE	NO.	TRANSACTION DESCRIPTION	✓	DEPOSIT		PAYMENT		509	95
7/30	417	Refined Oil Company				76	40	433	55
8/1	418	Jumpin' Pumpin' Aerobics				25	00	408	55
8/1		—Budget starts here—						408	55
8/4		Payroll		1136	15			1544	70
8/5	419	Ozzie's Office Supplies				14	30	1530	40
8/6	420	Smiley's Auto Finance Co.				276	12	1254	28

Figure 17: The Checking Account Entry for Check #420, a Car Payment

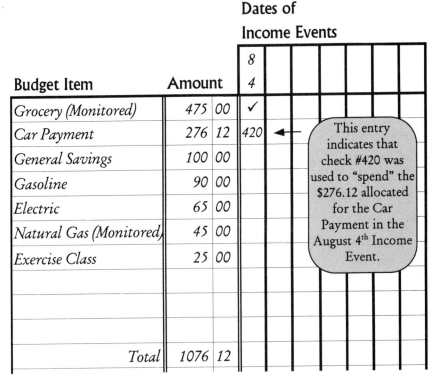

Figure 18: The Update to the Master Budget Sheet (First Part
of the Month) for Check #420, a Car Payment

> **Recap: Processing a Simple Budget Item**
>
> The check number is entered in the Master Budget
> Sheet.

Example: Bills Prior to Budget Start Date

A few days later, a telephone bill for $38.28 arrives. The pay-
ment is made in the usual way by writing a check and mailing it
off. This bill is for July's service. But since the family's budget
started on August 1st (see Figure 9), something special has to be

done *for this telephone bill only*. This expense occurred before the budget was started, and therefore no money has been allocated yet. Aside from the date of the bill (July) being prior to the starting date of the budget, this situation is further underscored by the fact that the Master Budget Sheet for the second part of the month, where the Telephone item is allocated, has not yet had an Income Event. The sheet is still blank and has no Income Event dates filled in. So, this one time, this bill has to be paid from the "$" Account—which is where all the checkbook money went in the first place. This "$" Account deduction is shown in Figure 19, and the checkbook entry for the check can be seen in Figure 20.

Date	Description	Amount		Balance	
				408	55
8/4	Payroll	+60	03	468	58
8/5	#419 Ozzie's Office Supplies	−14	30	454	28
8/10	#421 Telephone, pre-budget	−38	28	416	00

Figure 19: The "$" Account Entry for Check #421 for an Expense that Occurred before the Budget was Started

DATE	NO.	TRANSACTION DESCRIPTION	✓	DEPOSIT	PAYMENT	BALANCE 509 95	
7/30	417	Refined Oil Company			76 40	433	55
8/1	418	Jumpin' Pumpin' Aerobics			25 00	408	55
8/1		—Budget starts here—				408	55
8/4		Payroll		1136 15		1544	70
8/5	419	Ozzie's Office Supplies			14 30	1530	40
8/6	420	Smiley's Auto Finance Co.			276 12	1254	28
8/10	421	Yaquin Telephone			38 28	1216	00
8/12	422	Phude Groceries, Inc.			128 64	1087	36

Figure 20: The Checking Account Register Showing new Entries for Checks #421 and #422

Figure 20 also shows that the family went to the grocery store on August 12th and wrote check #422 for $128.64. This amount is deducted from the Grocery Monitored Account, as shown in Figure 21.

Date	Description	Amount	Balance	
8/4	Payroll	+475 00	475	00
8/12	#422 Phude Groceries, Inc.	−128 64	346	36

Figure 21: The Grocery Monitored Account Entry for Check #422

> **Recap: Bills Prior to Start Date of Budget**
>
> An entry was made in the "$" Account.

Example: Processing Your Bank Statement

At this point in time, the family receives its monthly checking account statement from the bank. In addition to the record of checks and deposits, the statement usually contains information about other credits and debits that occurred such as interest payments, automatic deposits and payments, and account charges. This new information has to be entered into the budget.

For this example, let's assume that there are two new transactions that have to be addressed. As you recall, the family has set things up so that their electric company bills are paid automatically by computer transfers from their checking account. One of the two new transactions is a confirmation of this bill payment. The other new item is an interest credit.

The first step is to record the entries in the checkbook register. This is shown in Figure 22. Starting with this figure we have tried to keep things simple by "scrolling the view" of the register and not showing some of the older entries at the top of the page.

DATE	NO.	TRANSACTION DESCRIPTION	✓	DEPOSIT		PAYMENT		BALANCE	
8/5	419	Ozzie's Office Supplies				14	30	1530	40
8/6	420	Smiley's Auto Finance Co.				276	12	1254	28
8/10	421	Yaquin Telephone				38	28	1216	00
8/12	422	Phude Groceries, Inc.				128	64	1087	36
7/22		Watt Power Co.(Autopay)				18	16	1069	20
8/1		Interest		5	38			1074	58

Figure 22: Updates to the Checking Account Register based on the Bank Statement

The date of the automatic payment for the electric bill, July 22nd, is once again before the August 1st budget start date. So this bill has to be taken from the "$" Account, *just this one time.* With this transaction, the budget has now caught up with all of the family's old bills. Everything from here on out is under the budget.

The interest payment is extra income, and is added directly to the "$" Account.

These two updates are shown in Figure 23.

Date	Description	Amount		Balance	
				408	55
8/4	Payroll	+60	03	468	58
8/5	#419 Ozzie's Office Supplies	–14	30	454	28
8/10	#421 Telephone, pre-budget	–38	28	416	00
7/22	Watt Power, pre-budget	–18	16	397	84
8/1	Interest	+5	38	403	22

Figure 23: Updates to the "$"Account based on the Bank Statement

> **Recap: Interest from Checking Account**
>
> An entry was made in the "$" Account.

Example: Monitored Budget Item

We have worked with the Grocery Monitored Account a couple of times; now let's do something with the Natural Gas Monitored Account. Suppose that a gas bill comes for $22.83. Being August, it is not surprising that this is low and under the budget amount of $45.00. For the Master Budget Sheet, the check number (#423) is entered at the intersection of the Natural Gas row and the August 4th Income Event column (see Figure 24). The remainder of $22.17 ($45.00 minus $22.83) is added into the Natural Gas Monitored Account, as shown in Figure 25.

Dates of
Income Events

Budget Item	Amount		8 4							
Grocery (Monitored)	475	00	✓							
Car Payment	276	12	420							
General Savings	100	00								
Gasoline	90	00								
Electric	65	00								
Natural Gas (Monitored)	45	00	423							
Exercise Class	25	00								
Total	1076	12								

Figure 24: The Update to the Master Budget Sheet (First Part of the Month) for Check #423, a Monitored Item

Date	Description	Amount		Balance	
8/16	#423, Bill Under Budget	+22	17	22	17

Figure 25: The Natural Gas Monitored Account Entry for Check #423

> **Recap: Processing a Monitored Budget Item**
>
> The check number is entered in the Master Budget Sheet, and the difference from the budgeted amount is entered in the Monitored Budget Account sheet.

Example: Next Income Event

A few weeks have now passed since the first Income Event, and it is time for another payday. This August 18th pay is the second Income Event of the month, and is entered on the second Master Budget Sheet. That sheet's total of $967.25 is subtracted from the pay amount of $1136.15; the remainder of $168.90 is added to the "$" Account. See Figure 26 through Figure 28 for these updates.

DATE	NO.	TRANSACTION DESCRIPTION	✓	DEPOSIT	PAYMENT	BALANCE
8/10	421	Yaquin Telephone			38 28	1216 00
8/12	422	Phude Groceries, Inc.			128 64	1087 36
7/22		Watt Power Co.(Autopay)			18 16	1069 20
8/1		Interest		5 38		1074 58
8/16	423	Liberty Northern Gaslines			22 83	1051 75
8/18		Payroll		1136 15		2187 90

Figure 26: August 18th Pay Entered into the Checkbook Register

Budget Item	Amount		Dates of Income Events 8 18							
House Payment	755	00								
General Savings	100	00								
Telephone	50	00								
Car Insurance	42	25								
Donations	20	00								
Total	967	25								

Figure 27: Income Event Entered into the Master Budget Sheet (Second Part of the Month) for the August 18th Pay

Date	Description	Amount		Balance 408	55
8/4	Payroll	+60	03	468	58
8/5	#419 Ozzie's Office Supplies	−14	30	454	28
8/10	#421 Telephone, pre-budget	−38	28	416	00
7/22	Watt Power, pre-budget	−18	16	397	84
8/1	Interest	+5	38	403	22
8/18	Payroll	+168	90	572	12

Figure 28: Update to the "$" Account for the August 18th Pay

> **Recap: Processing an Income Event**
>
> Enter a date on the Master Budget Sheet, perform a subtraction, and make an entry in the "$" Account.

Example: Bounded Budget Item & Multiple Bills

As one final example, let's simulate an evening bill-paying session and knock off three payments at once. Suppose that on August 22nd checks are made out for the mortgage, for $755.00; a bank card payment of $307.18; and a gasoline bill of $73.22. The house payment is a Simple Budget Item, all that has to be done is to enter the check number on the Master Budget Sheet. The bank card is handled by the family as unbudgeted expenses, so this total amount is deducted from the "$" Account. Finally, the "$" Account gets a nice bonus addition of $16.78, since the gasoline bill, a Bounded Budget Item, is under budget by that amount. Figure 29 through Figure 32 show the results of these updates.

DATE	NO.	TRANSACTION DESCRIPTION	✓	DEPOSIT	PAYMENT	BALANCE
7/22		Watt Power Co.(Autopay)			18 16	1069 20
8/1		Interest		5 38		1074 58
8/16	423	Liberty Northern Gaslines			22 83	1051 75
8/18		Payroll		1136 15		2187 90
8/22	424	ABC Mortgage Company			755 00	1432 90
8/22	425	MagicVista Bank Card			307 18	1125 72
8/22	426	Refined Oil Company			73 22	1052 50

Figure 29: The Checkbook Register After Paying Three Bills on August 22nd

Date	Description	Amount		Balance	
				408	55
8/4	Payroll	+60	03	468	58
8/5	#419 Ozzie's Office Supplies	−14	30	454	28
8/10	#421 Telephone, pre-budget	−38	28	416	00
7/22	Watt Power, pre-budget	−18	16	397	84
8/1	Interest	+5	38	403	22
8/18	Payroll	+168	90	572	12
8/22	#425 Bank Card	−307	18	264	94
8/22	#426 Gas Refund!	+16	78	281	72

Figure 30: The "$" Account After the August 22nd Bill Paying Session

Budget Item	Amount		Dates of Income Events							
			8 4							
Grocery (Monitored)	475	00	✓							
Car Payment	276	12	420							
General Savings	100	00								
Gasoline	90	00	426							
Electric	65	00								
Natural Gas (Monitored)	45	00	423							
Exercise Class	25	00								
Total	1076	12								

Figure 31: The Master Budget Sheet (First Part of the
Month) After the August 22nd Bill Paying Session

Budget Item	Amount		Dates of Income Events							
			8 18							
House Payment	755	00	424							
General Savings	100	00								
Telephone	50	00								
Car Insurance	42	25								
Donations	20	00								
Total	967	25								

Figure 32: The Master Budget Sheet (Second Part of the Month) After the August 22nd Bill Paying Session

> **Recap: Processing a Bounded Budget Item**
>
> The check number is entered in the Master Budget Sheet, and an entry is made in the "$" Account (in this case representing a refund!).

Summary

This chapter shows examples of how to get your budget started, enter money into it, check off each kind of budget item (simple, bounded, and monitored) in the Master Budget Sheet, work with Monitored Budget Accounts, and work with the "$" Account. Though there were a number of pages here with "clips" of the

BudgetYes sheets showing each stage of the process, perhaps making it seem like an involved process, we hope you see that it is actually very quick and easy to enter items into your budget. As mentioned earlier, it took a few pages to show these simple actions, but it only takes a moment to do when you pay your bills.

The next chapter provides some further exercises for you to try, with the answers given in Chapter 11. If you've got the hang of it, head on to Chapter 12!

10

Exercises

Some people feel that they learn best by doing, and ask for a chance to practice using the BudgetYes system. If you are interested, a description of events in the life of our hypothetical family is presented below. For each event, you can practice making the corresponding entries in their budget, continuing on from the state of the budget in the last chapter. The answers are given in the next chapter.

- ✓ The family takes a trip to the grocery store on August 27th, and writes Check #427 for $198.96.

- ✓ On August 30th, the exercise class fee of $25.00 is paid by Check #428, made out to "Jumpin' Pumpin' Aerobics."

- ✓ September 1st is a payday.

✓ Someone takes another trip to the grocery store on September 4th, and this time spends $246.87 with Check #429.

✓ The car payment is made on September 7th with Check #430.

✓ The telephone bill of $45.25 is paid on September 9th using Check #431.

✓ Also on September 9th, Aunt Marge sends a birthday gift of $50.00, which is promptly deposited in the checking account.

✓ On September 11th, another checking account statement is received from the bank. This statement lists the following credits and debits:
  ✓ There was an automatic transfer of $100.00 to the savings account on August 15th.
  ✓ On August 22nd, there was an automatic payment of $77.12 to the Watt Power Company.
  ✓ There was another automatic transfer of $100.00 to the savings account on August 30th.
  ✓ There was an interest payment of $2.46 on September 1st.
  ✓ A "Printed Check Fee" of $4.50 showed up on September 5th to pay for the new checks the family ordered.

Summary

These exercises covered the most common actions you'll perform when running BudgetYes. The answers follow...

11

Answers to Exercises

The previous chapter included descriptions of several events that you could use as practice exercises. These events are repeated below, with each followed by a description, in italics, of how it was entered into the family's budget system. Following that are the figures that show the final state of the budget.

✓ The family takes a trip to the grocery store on August 27th, and writes Check #427 for $198.96.

$198.96 should be deducted from the Grocery Monitored Account, leaving $147.40.

✓ On August 30th, the exercise class fee of $25.00 is paid by Check #428, made out to "Jumpin' Pumpin' Aerobics."

The number "428" should be entered on the Master Budget Sheet for the first part of the month, in the first box of the "Exercise Class" row.

✓ September 1st is a payday.

Three steps are required: (1) The date of "9/1" should be entered in the second box on the "Dates of Income Events" row; (2) $475 should be transferred to the Grocery Monitored Account (for a new balance of $622.40), and a check mark placed on the Master Budget Sheet, in the next empty box of the "Grocery" row, to indicate that the money was transferred; and (3) The $60.03 difference between the pay amount of $1136.15 and the $1076.12 total on the Master Budget Sheet should be added to the "$" Account for a new total there of $341.75.

✓ Someone takes another trip to the grocery store on September 4th, and this time spends $246.87 with Check #429.

$246.87 should be deducted from the Grocery Monitored Account, leaving $375.53.

✓ The car payment is made on September 7th with Check #430.

The number "430" should be entered on the Master Budget Sheet for the first part of the month, in the second box of the "Car Payment" row.

✓ The telephone bill of $45.25 is paid on September 9th using Check #431.

The number "431" should be entered on the Master Budget Sheet for the second part of the month, in the first box of the "Telephone" row. Also, since this bill is $4.75 under the budgeted amount of $50.00, the "$" Account gets an addition for a new total of $346.50.

✓ Also on September 9th, Aunt Marge sends a birthday gift of $50.00, which is promptly deposited in the checking account.

This extra money goes exactly where it should—into the family's spending money as an addition to the "$" Account. The new total of the account is $396.50.

✓ On September 11th, another checking account statement is received from the bank. This statement lists the following credits and debits:

   ✓ There was an automatic transfer of $100.00 to the savings account on August 15th.

*   The date of "8/15" should be entered on the Master Budget Sheet for the first part of the month, in the first box of the "General Savings" row.*

   ✓ On August 22nd, there was an automatic payment of $77.12 to the Watt Power Company.

*   The date of "8/22" should be entered on the Master Budget Sheet for the first part of the month, in the first box of the "Electric" row. Also, since this bill was over budget, $12.12 should be deducted from the "$" Account, for a balance there of $384.38.*

✓ There was another automatic transfer of $100.00 to the savings account on August 30th.

The date of "8/30" should be entered on the Master Budget Sheet for the first part of the month, in the second box of the "General Savings" row.

✓ There was an interest payment of $2.46 on September 1st.

The $2.46 should be added to the "$" Account for a new balance of $386.84.

✓ A "Printed Check Fee" of $4.50 showed up on September 5th to pay for the new checks the family ordered.

This unbudgeted expense should be deducted from the "$" Account for a new balance of $382.34.

Final State of the Budget, After the Exercises

The final state of the checkbook register, the two Master Budget Sheets, the "$" Account, and the Grocery Monitored Account after all the above transactions have been entered are shown in Figure 33 through Figure 37.

DATE	NO.	TRANSACTION DESCRIPTION	✓	DEPOSIT		PAYMENT		BALANCE	
8/22	426	Refined Oil Company				73	22	1052	50
8/27	427	Phude Groceries, Inc.				198	96	853	54
8/30	428	Jumpin' Pumpin' Aerobics				25	00	828	54
9/1		Payroll		1136	15			1964	69
9/4	429	Phude Groceries, Inc.				246	87	1717	82
9/7	430	Smiley's Auto Finance Co.				276	12	1441	70
9/9	431	Yaquin Telephone				45	25	1396	45
9/9		Birthday Gift—Aunt Marge		50	00			1446	45
8/15		Transfer to Savings				100	00	1346	45
8/22		Watt Power Co.(Autopay)				77	12	1269	33
8/30		Transfer to Savings				100	00	1169	33
9/1		Interest		2	46			1171	79
9/5		Printed Check Fee				4	50	1167	29

Figure 33: The Checkbook Register as of September 11th
(after all exercises are completed)

Dates of

Income Events

Budget Item	Amount		8 4	9 1						
Grocery (Monitored)	475	00	✓	✓						
Car Payment	276	12	420	430						
General Savings	100	00	8/15							
Gasoline	90	00	426							
Electric	65	00	8/22							
Natural Gas (Monitored)	45	00	423							
Exercise Class	25	00	428							
Total	1076	12								

Figure 34: The Master Budget Sheet (First Part of the Month) as of September 11th (after all exercises are completed)

Budget Item	Amount		Dates of Income Events 8 18						
House Payment	755	00	424						
General Savings	100	00	8/30						
Telephone	50	00	431						
Car Insurance	42	25							
Donations	20	00							
Total	967	25							

Figure 35: The Master Budget Sheet (Second Part of the Month) as of September 11th (after all exercises are completed)

Date	Description	Amount		Balance	
				408	55
8/4	Payroll	+60	03	468	58
8/5	#419 Ozzie's Office Supplies	-14	30	454	28
8/10	#421 Telephone, pre-budget	-38	28	416	00
7/22	Watt Power, pre-budget	-18	16	397	84
8/1	Interest	+5	38	403	22
8/18	Payroll	+168	90	572	12
8/22	#425 Bank Card	-307	18	264	94
8/22	#426 Gas Refund!	+16	78	281	72
9/1	Payroll	+60	03	341	75
9/9	#431 Telephone Refund!	+4	75	346	50
9/9	Aunt Marge's Gift	+50	00	396	50
8/22	Electric—Over Budget	-12	12	384	38
9/1	Interest	+2	46	386	84
9/5	Printed Check Fee	-4	50	382	34

Figure 36: The "$" Account as of September 11th (after all exercises are completed)

Date	Description	Amount		Balance	
8/4	Payroll	+475	00	475	00
8/12	#422 Phude Groceries, Inc.	−128	64	346	36
8/27	#427 Phude Groceries, Inc.	−198	96	147	40
9/1	Payroll	+475	00	622	40
9/4	#429 Phude Groceries, Inc.	−246	87	375	53
9/12	#427 Phude Groceries, Inc.	−82	34	293	19

Figure 37: The Grocery Monitored Account as of September 11th (after all exercises are completed)

Summary

How did you do? For even more examples, see the next chapter.

12

Three Month Example Budget

For those who would like even further examples, this chapter presents a complete record of the family's checkbook register and budgeting system for over three months, beginning with the start of the budget on August 1st and continuing well into October.

In preparation for some concepts that will be explained in upcoming chapters, two new things have been included in the examples below. One is that the word "Reconciled" appears in several places. The other is the concept of a "triple" pay that occurs on September 29th. These things are included in the examples so that when you learn about them in later chapters, you can refer back to this complete budget and see them working in context.

DATE	NO.	TRANSACTION DESCRIPTION	✓	DEPOSIT		PAYMENT		BALANCE 509	95
7/30	417	Refined Oil Company				76	40	433	55
8/1	418	Jumpin' Pumpin' Aerobics				25	00	408	55
8/1		—Budget starts here—						408	55
8/4		Payroll		1136	15			1544	70
8/5	419	Ozzie's Office Supplies				14	30	1530	40
8/6	420	Smiley's Auto Finance Co.				276	12	1254	28
8/10	421	Yaquin Telephone				38	28	1216	00
8/12	422	Phude Groceries, Inc.				128	64	1087	36
7/22		Watt Power Co.(Autopay)				18	16	1069	20
8/1		Interest		5	38			1074	58
8/14		—Reconciled—						1074	58
8/16	423	Liberty Northern Gaslines				22	83	1051	75
8/18		Payroll		1136	15			2187	90
8/22	424	ABC Mortgage Company				755	00	1432	90
8/22	425	MagicVista Bank Card				307	18	1125	72
8/22	426	Refined Oil Company				73	22	1052	50
8/27	427	Phude Groceries, Inc.				198	96	853	54
8/30	428	Jumpin' Pumpin' Aerobics				25	00	828	54
9/1		Payroll		1136	15			1964	69
9/4	429	Phude Groceries, Inc.				246	87	1717	82
9/7	430	Smiley's Auto Finance Co.				276	12	1441	70
9/9	431	Yaquin Telephone				45	25	1396	45
9/9		Birthday Gift—Aunt Marge		50	00			1446	45
8/15		Transfer to Savings				100	00	1346	45
8/22		Watt Power Co.(Autopay)				77	12	1269	33
8/30		Transfer to Savings				100	00	1169	33
9/1		Interest		2	46			1171	79
9/5		Printed Check Fee				4	50	1167	29
9/11		—Reconciled—						1167	29

Figure 38: The First Page of the Checkbook Register for the Complete Three Month Example

DATE	NO.	TRANSACTION DESCRIPTION	✓	DEPOSIT	PAYMENT	BALANCE 1167	29
9/12	432	Phude Groceries, Inc.			82 34	1084	95
9/15		Payroll		1136 15		2221	10
9/16	433	Liberty Northern Gaslines			11 01	2210	09
9/16	434	MagicVista Bank Card			128 68	2081	41
9/16	435	ABC Mortgage Company			755 00	1326	41
9/23	436	Refined Oil Company			82 70	1243	71
9/23	437	Phude Groceries, Inc.			163 27	1080	44
9/27	438	Jumpin' Pumpin' Aerobics			25 00	1055	44
9/29		Payroll—Triple!!!		1136 15		2191	59
9/30	439	Sam & Sam's Stereo Shop			505 41	1686	18
10/7	440	Phude Groceries, Inc.			78 05	1608	13
10/10	441	Smiley's Auto Finance Co.			276 12	1332	01
10/13		Payroll		1136 15		2468	16
10/13	442	Yaquin Telephone			39 98	2428	18
10/13	443	Halloween Show Tickets			26 50	2401	68
10/13	444	Liberty Northern Gaslines			49 18	2352	50
9/15		Transfer to Savings			100 00	2252	50
9/22		Watt Power Co.(Autopay)			62 28	2190	22
9/30		Transfer to Savings			100 00	2090	22
10/1		Interest		3 37		2093	59
10/13		—Reconciled—				2093	59
10/18	445	MagicVista Bank Card			360 12	1733	47
10/20	446	Bicycle Blitz for Charity			40 00	1693	47

Figure 39: The Second Page of the Checkbook Register for the Complete Three Month Example

Dates of
Income Events

Budget Item	Amount		8 4	9 1	10 13				
Grocery (Monitored)	475	00	✓	✓	✓				
Car Payment	276	12	420	430	441				
General Savings	100	00	8/15	9/15					
Gasoline	90	00	426	436					
Electric	65	00	8/22	9/22					
Natural Gas (Monitored)	45	00	423	433	444				
Exercise Class	25	00	428	438					
Total	1076	12							

Figure 40: The Master Budget Sheet (First Part of the
Month) Register for the Complete Three Month Example

Budget Item	Amount		Dates of Income Events							
			8	9						
			18	15						
House Payment	755	00	424	435						
General Savings	100	00	8/30	9/30						
Telephone	50	00	431	442						
Car Insurance	42	25								
Donations	20	00	446	→						
Total	967	25								

Figure 41: The Master Budget Sheet (Second Part of the Month) Register for the Complete Three Month Example

Date	Description	Amount		Balance 408	55
8/4	Payroll	+60	03	468	58
8/5	#419 Ozzie's Office Supplies	−14	30	454	28
8/10	#421 Telephone, pre-budget	−38	28	416	00
7/22	Watt Power, pre-budget	−18	16	397	84
8/1	Interest	+5	38	403	22
8/14	—Reconciled—				
8/18	Payroll	+168	90	572	12
8/22	#425 Bank Card	−307	18	264	94
8/22	#426 Gas Refund!	+16	78	281	72
9/1	Payroll	+60	03	341	75
9/9	#431 Telephone Refund!	+4	75	346	50
9/9	Aunt Marge's Gift	+50	00	396	50
8/22	Electric—Over Budget	−12	12	384	38
9/1	Interest	+2	46	386	84
9/5	Printed Check Fee	−4	50	382	34
9/11	—Reconciled—				
9/15	Payroll	+168	90	551	24
9/16	#434 Bank Card	−128	68	422	56
9/23	#436 Gasoline Refund!	+7	30	429	86
9/29	Payroll—Triple!!!	+1136	15	1566	01
9/30	#439 Stereo	−505	41	1060	60
10/9	Transfer (Natural Gas)	−50	00	1010	60
10/13	Payroll	+60	03	1070	63
10/13	#442 Telephone Refund!	+10	02	1080	65
10/13	#443 Halloween Show	−26	50	1054	15
9/22	Electric Refund!	+2	72	1056	87
10/1	Interest	+3	37	1060	24
10/13	—Reconciled—				
10/18	#445 Bank Card	−360	12	700	12

Figure 42: The "$" Account for the Complete Three Month Example

Date	Description	Amount		Balance	
8/4	Payroll	+475	00	475	00
8/12	#422 Phude Groceries, Inc.	-128	64	346	36
8/14	—Reconciled—				
8/27	#427 Phude Groceries, Inc.	-198	96	147	40
9/1	Payroll	+475	00	622	40
9/4	#429 Phude Groceries, Inc.	-246	87	375	53
9/12	#432 Phude Groceries, Inc.	-82	34	293	19
9/11	—Reconciled—				
9/23	#437 Phude Groceries, Inc.	-163	27	129	92
10/7	#440 Phude Groceries, Inc.	-78	05	51	87
10/13	Payroll	+475	00	526	87
10/13	—Reconciled—				

Figure 43: The Grocery Monitored Account for the Complete Three Month Example

| | | | Balance |
Date	Description	Amount	
8/16	#423, Bill Under Budget	+22 17	22 17
9/11	—Reconciled—		
9/16	#433, Bill Under Budget	+33 99	56 16
10/9	Transfer from $ Account	+50 00	106 16
10/13	#444, Bill Over Budget	-4 18	101 98
10/13	—Reconciled—		

Figure 44: The Natural Gas Monitored Account for the
Complete Three Month Example

Summary

Now that you are an expert, read on to learn how to *reconcile* the
BudgetYes system with your checkbook!

13

Reconciling

As has been mentioned several times in the preceding chapters, the basic concept behind the BudgetYes system is that it is an *overlay* of your checking account. It is a tool that allows you to see at a glance how you have decided to allocate the money in your checkbook register.

Because of the way your checkbook balance and budgeting system work hand-in-hand, it is important and helpful to check every so often to ensure that they are still in synch, and that the budget is still overlaying the correct amounts. In other words, the amount of money shown in your BudgetYes sheets should match your checkbook balance. This verification process is called *reconciling*.

> *Reconciling* is the verification process you use to
> ensure your checkbook balance and your
> BudgetYes system are still in synch with one
> another. The process of reconciling can point out
> errors in your checkbook, or budget, entries and
> transactions.

The Mechanics of Reconciliation

When you implement the BudgetYes system, you effectively "divide up" the money in your checkbook into categories that you choose. Some of the money is "held" in items in the Master Budget Sheets, some goes into the "$" Account, and some is distributed across various Monitored Budget Accounts.

The process of reconciliation is simply a verification that all of the various allocations still add up to your current checkbook balance. That is the goal, because BudgetYes overlays the checkbook. The amounts represented in each should be equal.

One way to reconcile is to add up all of the amounts in the various portions of your budget, and compare that total with the balance in your checkbook. Another way, which is really just the flip side of the same coin, is to start with the checkbook balance, subtract all the budget allocations, and check to make sure that the result is zero.

The method that we recommend, and the one that will be explained in this book, is the second, where you begin with your checkbook balance. The reason is that this method often makes errors much easier to find. But, we are getting a little ahead of ourselves. Let's look at the steps of reconciliation, go through an example, and then talk about finding errors.

Four Steps to Reconciling Your Budget

1. Start with your checkbook balance.

2. Subtract the current balances of all Monitored Budget Accounts (including the "$" Account).

3. Subtract all "empty" cells on the Master Budget Sheets ("empty" cells are those that have an Income Event date above them, but no mark inside them).

4. The result should be zero.

A Reconciliation Example

Let's go through an example of a reconciliation, using the complete budget record presented in the previous chapter. If you have a calculator handy, you may find it useful to follow along as we proceed.

Step #1: The first step is to start with your checkbook balance. When we left off following our example family's budget, their checkbook showed a balance of $1693.47, as shown in Figure 45. Enter 1693.47 into your calculator, and the first step is completed.

DATE	NO.	TRANSACTION DESCRIPTION	✓	DEPOSIT	PAYMENT	BALANCE
9/15		Transfer to Savings			100 00	2252 50
9/22		Watt Power Co.(Autopay)			62 28	2190 22
9/30		Transfer to Savings			100 00	2090 22
10/1		Interest		3 37		2093 59
10/13		—Reconciled—				2093 59
10/18	445	MagicVista Bank Card			360 12	1733 47
10/20	446	Bicycle Blitz for Charity			40 00	1693 47

Figure 45: The Checkbook Register Showing an Ending Balance of $1693.47

Step #2: The next step is to subtract the current balances of all Monitored Budget Accounts. This includes the "$" Account, since, as we have stated before, it is just a very special Monitored Budget Account. Let's start with the "$" Account. As shown in Figure 46, its current balance is $700.12. Subtracting that from the total in your calculator should leave you with $993.35.

Date	Description	Amount		Balance	
				408	55
8/4	Payroll	+60	03	468	58
8/5	#419 Ozzie's Office Supplies	−14	30	454	28
8/10	#421 Telephone, pre-budget	−38	28	416	00
7/22	Watt Power, pre-budget	−18	16	397	84
8/1	Interest	+5	38	403	22
8/14	—Reconciled—				
8/18	Payroll	+168	90	572	12
8/22	#425 Bank Card	−307	18	264	94
8/22	#426 Gas Refund!	+16	78	281	72
9/1	Payroll	+60	03	341	75
9/9	#431 Telephone Refund!	+4	75	346	50
9/9	Aunt Marge's Gift	+50	00	396	50
8/22	Electric—Over Budget	−12	12	384	38
9/1	Interest	+2	46	386	84
9/5	Printed Check Fee	−4	50	382	34
9/11	—Reconciled—				
9/15	Payroll	+168	90	551	24
9/16	#434 Bank Card	−128	68	422	56
9/23	#436 Gasoline Refund!	+7	30	429	86
9/29	Payroll—Triple!!!	+1136	15	1566	01
9/30	#439 Stereo	−505	41	1060	60
10/9	Transfer (Natural Gas)	−50	00	1010	60
10/13	Payroll	+60	03	1070	63
10/13	#442 Telephone Refund!	+10	02	1080	65
10/13	#443 Halloween Show	−26	50	1054	15
9/22	Electric Refund!	+2	72	1056	87
10/1	Interest	+3	37	1060	24
10/13	—Reconciled—				
10/18	#445 Bank Card	−360	12	700	12

Figure 46: The "$" Account Showing an Ending Balance of $700.12

The Grocery Monitored Account has a balance of $526.87, as shown in Figure 47. Subtracting that figure from the running total in the calculator leaves $466.48.

Date	Description	Amount		Balance	
8/4	Payroll	+475	00	475	00
8/12	#422 Phude Groceries, Inc.	−128	64	346	36
8/14	—Reconciled—				
8/27	#427 Phude Groceries, Inc.	−198	96	147	40
9/1	Payroll	+475	00	622	40
9/4	#429 Phude Groceries, Inc.	−246	87	375	53
9/12	#432 Phude Groceries, Inc.	−82	34	293	19
9/11	—Reconciled—				
9/23	#437 Phude Groceries, Inc.	−163	27	129	92
10/7	#440 Phude Groceries, Inc.	−78	05	51	87
10/13	Payroll	+475	00	526	87

Figure 47: The Grocery Monitored Account Showing an Ending Balance of $526.87

Finally, the Natural Gas Monitored Account has a balance of $101.98, as shown in Figure 48. Deducting $101.98 from the calculator total of $466.48 leaves $364.50.

Date	Description	Amount		Balance	
8/16	#423, Bill Under Budget	+22	17	22	17
9/11	—Reconcile—				
9/16	#433, Bill Under Budget	+33	99	56	16
10/9	Transfer from $ Account	+50	00	106	16
10/13	#444, Bill Over Budget	–4	18	101	98

Figure 48: The Natural Gas Monitored Account Showing an Ending Balance of $101.98

Step #3: The next step is to subtract all "empty" cells on all Master Budget Sheets. A word of explanation is in order here. Given a typical Master Budget Sheet, there will be lots of cells that appear to be "empty." But the only empty cells that should be subtracted during the reconciliation process are those that have an Income Event date above them. Recall that the entering of an Income Event date "energizes" or "activates" all the cells underneath the date. During a reconciliation, you only want to count the activated cells.

If you examine the Master Budget Sheet for the first part of the month shown in Figure 49, you will find four empty cells. All of them occur in the final completed column, the one for the October 13th Income Event. The four empty cells correspond to General Savings, Gasoline, Electric, and the Exercise Class. Each corresponding amount has to be subtracted from the running tally in the calculator. So, subtracting $100.00, $90.00, $65.00 and $25.00 should leave you with $84.50. We are almost done!

Budget Item	Amount		Dates of Income Events							
			8	9	10					
			4	1	13					
Grocery (Monitored)	475	00	✓	✓	✓					
Car Payment	276	12	420	430	441					
General Savings	100	00	8/15	9/15						
Gasoline	90	00	426	436						
Electric	65	00	8/22	9/22						
Natural Gas (Monitored)	45	00	423	433	444					
Exercise Class	25	00	428	438						
Total	1076	12								

Figure 49: The Master Budget Sheet for the First Part of the Month, Showing Four Empty Cells

The last item to process is the Master Budget Sheet for the second part of the month, which is shown in Figure 50. This sheet contains two empty cells, both corresponding to the Car Insurance item. (The family is using this item to save up for their semiannual payment. This way, they will not be hit with a huge payment twice a year—the money will be there waiting for them.) The two cells each have a value of $42.25. Subtracting $42.25, twice, from the current calculator tally of $84.50 leaves...zero!

Step #4: That's right, the result was zero, the account is reconciled!

| | | Dates of Income Events | | | | | | | |
| | | 8 | 9 | | | | | | |
Budget Item	Amount	18	15						
House Payment	755	00	424	435					
General Savings	100	00	8/30	9/30					
Telephone	50	00	431	442					
Car Insurance	42	25							
Donations	20	00	446	→					
Total	967	25							

Figure 50: The Master Budget Sheet for the Second Part of
the Month, Showing Two Empty Cells

Things That Go Wrong

Occasionally, it will happen that something other than a zero
will be smiling up at you when you complete the reconciliation
process. This means your budget did not reconcile, and there is
an error somewhere.

This section presents some tips on what possible errors might be,
where to look for them, and how to find them. (These errors are
all thoroughly tested; we've made every one of them! ☺)

We have tried to list these items in priority order, meaning that the first one is the most common, the second, the next-most common, and so on.

A missed entry. A missed entry is something that is in the checkbook that is not in the budget, or vice-versa. In other words, this is an entry that has been made in one place but not the other. You may have written a check and forgotten to deduct it from your "$" Account, or placed a check number in a Master Budget Sheet cell but forgotten to write the corresponding entry in your checkbook ledger.

Fortunately, these errors are usually easy to find, because the amount left in the calculator after the reconciliation is done will point to the guilty culprit.

Clue #1: Suppose that our hypothetical family had just performed a reconciliation, and the calculator showed a balance of $267.12. Well, that's the car payment amount! Something was not entered correctly for the car payment. Suppose the final balance was $755.00. Recognize that? Of course, it is the house payment. You can usually zero in on these types of errors quite quickly.

Clue #2: Furthermore, the final tally in your calculator can be either a positive or a negative amount, and this can give you another clue. For example, if a mistake were made with the house payment, the amount in the calculator after a reconciliation might either be "755.00" or "-755.00". If the amount is positive (greater than zero), it usually means that the entry was made in the budget but is missing from the checkbook. If the amount is negative (less than zero), it is usually just the opposite—the checkbook has an entry that the budget does not.

By the way, it is this common type of error that makes us recommend the reconciliation method that we do, where you start with your checkbook balance and subtract away all budget amounts. Doing it this way means that the only thing left in your calculator will be the errors—and they will often give themselves away!

Arithmetic errors. This is the same nemesis that you may now encounter in your checkbook register: just adding or subtracting wrong. Check the arithmetic, not only in your checkbook, but also in the Monitored Budget Account Sheets. If you find something that does not add up right, correct the error and do the reconciliation again.

 TIP: A frustrating note is that an arithmetic error can occur during the reconciliation process itself. There might not be a darn thing wrong with either your checkbook or your budget, but if you enter an incorrect number or jam your finger between two keys on the calculator, it will look as though something is wrong. Sometimes, it pays just to do the reconciliation over again.

Many people will find that use of the BudgetYes system will actually help them to keep their checkbook balanced. Instead of only a monthly bank statement to use as a benchmark, reconciliation provides additional verification whenever needed. The level of control the BudgetYes system affords you will often lend additional accuracy, helping things to balance out.

Transposed numbers. The human mind sometimes has a tendency to flip pairs of numbers around. When running the BudgetYes system, you often have to make the same entry in two different places, for example, in your checkbook register and in the "$" Account. Sometimes, you will find mysterious gremlins will transpose two digits of what should be identical numbers. You might find "$18.59" in your checkbook, and "$18.95" in your "$" Account[5]. The key to finding these gremlins is to cross-check your entries, and make sure that the same value is entered in the budget for every entry in the checkbook.

Inconsistent entries. This type of troublemaker is a more general case of the previous item. Any time that an entry made within the budget does not agree with the corresponding entry in the checkbook, the reconciliation will fail.

There are lots of different mistakes that can cause these inconsistencies. The wrong cell in a Master Budget Sheet can be marked. The previous month's amount might accidentally be copied from a bill. The wrong line of a checkbook might be referenced. An entry can be made on the wrong Monitored Account. Or the check number (such as #1234) can be entered as the amount ($12.34).

The way to find these errors, as with the special case of transposed numbers, is to verify all entries, making sure that everything agrees and is entered in the correct place.

Multiple errors. Yes, it can happen that there is more than one error in your checkbook or budget. You might reconcile, get a non-zero answer, find and fix an error, reconcile again, and then have a *different* non-zero answer. Arrrgh!

---

[5] For our readers who are math whizzes or are intrigued by number tricks, we point out that when there is a transposition error, the total of the digits in the final calculator tally will be a multiple of nine. So, if after a reconciliation your calculator shows a number such as "18" or "-0.27" or "3.60", suspect that you might have a transposition error. This works because of a phenomenon known as "casting out nines", a natural law that gives special properties to the highest single digit of our base-10 numbering system.

The frustrating thing about multiple errors is that they can hide one another. One might be positive, and another negative, so that they nearly cancel one another out. Or, two totals you are familiar with (such as the $267.12 in our examples for the car payment, and the $755.00 for the house payment) might combine, when added together in your calculator, to something that doesn't ring any bells ("Where did $1022.12 come from?")

The only thing you can do is start looking for errors. Check your arithmetic. Look for inconsistent entries. Make sure that the correct cells have been marked on the Master Budget Sheets. Look at the pennies for clues (for example, in the $1022.12 total cited in the last paragraph, the 12 cents in pennies might tip you off that the car payment is involved).

Every time you find an error, reconcile again. The new tally in the calculator might give you more hints as to where to look. Or, you might finally come down to a familiar value that will give itself away.

At any rate, good luck finding those errors! With time and practice, you will make fewer and fewer errors, and when gremlins do creep in, you will find them quickly.

How Strict Should You Be?

One final note. A reasonable question is how much of your time this is all worth—if your budget is off by 7 cents, is it worth spending hours trying to find the error? No, of course not. Remember, a budget is a tool, not a dictator.

If your budget does not reconcile, it is usually worth a look to find the error. Most mistakes pop out quickly. It is also worth verifying that something major is not wrong. (Once, to cite a personal example, we had a reconciliation that was off by just a few dollars. A quick check showed that there were two errors, over a hundred dollars each, that canceled one another out. We were glad we spent the few moments to look into that!) But once you have looked at the obvious things, checked a few additions, and cross-checked your most recent transactions, you have better things to do with your time. Make an adjustment in your "$" Account to make your budget happy again, and get on with things.

Mark Your Reconciliation Points!

When your budget is reconciled, and you have that nice, squeaky-clean zero displayed on your calculator, please do yourself a favor and mark your checkbook register, and all your Monitored Accounts, at the point at which the reconciliation occurred.

You can mark your reconciliation points by simply drawing a line after the last entry in each account, and entering the date. Or, put the word "Reconciled" as the next entry in the account. You might even consider using a different colored pencil, marker, or highlight color so that the reconciliation points stand out.

If you look back at the complete three-month budgeting record in the previous chapter, you will see examples of marked reconciliation points scattered throughout the checkbook register and the Monitored Accounts.

Marking your reconciliation points saves you work later on when you are looking for an error. When you try a new reconciliation and it fails, you know that you only have to back up to the last checkpoint to find the mistake. So, rather than checking dozens of entries for arithmetic errors, transposed numbers, and missed entries, just go back to your last reconciliation mark and start from there.

Some readers might even find it useful to mark their Master Budget Sheets at reconciliation points, and there are lots of techniques that can be used. When you complete an entire Income Event column, you could place a check mark above it, or draw a colored line to the right of it. You could lightly shade in all completed cells when a reconciliation occurs. Or photocopy your sheets when they reconcile, and place the date on the photocopy. Some folks might even find it useful to make entries in their budget (both on the Master Budget Sheets and on the Monitored Budget Accounts) in different colored pencils, with each color corresponding to a reconciliation period. You can do as much or as little as you like, depending on how much trouble you experience when reconciling. Make it easy on yourself by using the system with which you feel the most comfortable.

How Often Should You Reconcile?

Like the marking of your budget at reconciliation points, the frequency with which you reconcile is a personal choice based on how comfortable you feel with the system and how often you make mistakes. Reconciliation can be done at any time, so you can do it as often as you wish.

When you are first starting the BudgetYes system, we suggest that just for the first two or three transactions, you reconcile after every entry. (In other words, make an entry, and then reconcile. Make another entry, and then reconcile.) This exercise will really drive home how the reconciliation process works, demonstrate how monies flow in and out of the budget and checkbook, and cement the concept of how your budget overlays and mirrors every penny in your checking account.

TIP: After the initial exercise, there are two "classic" times that you might consider reconciling. One is when you process your monthly checking account statement. At that point, you go through the process of making sure that everything is in agreement with your financial institution, and it is a logical time to make sure that everything is in synch with your budget, as well.

The other time it makes sense to reconcile is after a bill-paying session. Many people save up their bills, and then pay several at once on a weekday evening, or Saturday morning, or whenever. If you sit down to make several checkbook transactions, finish clean and tidy by doing a reconcile.

Summary

It is necessary to keep your BudgetYes sheets and checkbook balance in synch with one another. The BudgetYes system *overlays* your checkbook to give you a visual picture of your finances. The amount of money BudgetYes shows must match your checkbook.

Reconciling is an easy four step process: enter your checkbook balance in your calculator, then subtract the current balances of all Monitored Accounts, then subtract all "empty" cells on the Master Budget Sheets, and your result should be zero! Watch out for one of the things that might go wrong: a missed entry, an arithmetic error, transposed numbers, inconsistent entries, or multiple errors!

Most of all, after you have reconciled, mark that location in your checkbook and BudgetYes sheets, so you know where the budget was last correct if you come up with a future error.

14

Changes to Your Budget

Things change. You can switch jobs. You can commit to a major new purchase, such as a new home. You can receive a raise, or be saddled with a cutback. People will move in and out of your household. Your rent can go up. You might even move across the country.

Sooner or later, probably sooner, you will want to update your budget to reflect the changes in your life.

Begin Again

There are three basic ways to make changes to your budget. The first of these is to simply start over. Since you can begin the BudgetYes system at any time, you can always draw up a new budget, new Master Budget Sheets, new Monitored Budget

Accounts, and an "empty" "$" Account, and make it effective immediately. Copy your checkbook balance over into the new "$" Account, and your new budget is up and rolling. This method gives you a clean break, allowing you to start from scratch.

Phase in New Master Budget Sheets

The second method provides a cleaner transition from one phase of your budget to the next. To accomplish this adjustment, create new Master Budget Sheets, reflecting your new budget plan, and make them take effect at your next Income Event. In other words, you place the date of your next Income Event on the new Master Budget Sheet instead of the next empty column of the old one. That is all there is to it! The new Master Budget Sheet has been phased in.

If there are any empty cells on the old Master Budget Sheets, you will need to keep them "in play" until they are completely filled up. At that point, the transition to the new budget will be complete.

Making Minor Adjustments

The final method for adjusting your budget can be employed when you only need to make a small tweak, or minor adjustment, to a budget item or two. To make this happen, end one row on your Master Budget Sheet and begin using a new, replacement row.

Let's look at an example. Suppose that our hypothetical family wanted to begin budgeting $100.00 per month for gasoline, up from the $90.00 they are currently setting aside. Figure 51 shows how they might accomplish this. A new row for the Gasoline item, with the new $100 amount, is added to the appropriate Master Budget Sheet. Then, the remaining cells in the original row are filled with X's, indicating they will no longer be used. Ditto with the cells in the new row that correspond to Income Events in the past.

Finally, a new total is computed for the items in the Master Budget Sheet. That's it—the new gasoline amount will take effect at the next Income Event.

			Dates of Income Events						
Budget Item	Amount		8 4	9 1	10 13				
Grocery (Monitored)	475	00	✓	✓	✓				
Car Payment	276	12	420	430	441				
General Savings	100	00	8/15	9/15					
~~Gasoline~~	90	00	426	436		✘	✘	✘	✘
Electric	65	00	8/22	9/22					
Natural Gas (Monitored)	45	00	423	433	444				
Exercise Class	25	00	428	438					
Gasoline	100	00	✘	✘	✘				
Total	~~1076~~	~~12~~							
Total	1086	12							

Figure 51: A Master Budget Sheet Showing a Budget Adjustment

Note that the family still has one cell corresponding to the old $90 amount to use up. This happened because they decided to adjust their budget before their most recent bill was paid. When the check for October's gasoline bill is made out, that last cell should be "spent." Everything will then be set for the next Income Event. We illustrated the budget adjustment in this way to emphasize that you really can change your budget at any time: just be aware of which Income Events have occurred, and which bills have been paid. In particular, don't try to change the value of a Master Budget Sheet cell whose Income Event has already occurred. Your budget won't reconcile unless you account for the change.

Monitored Budget Account Transfers

We sneaked in an example of an account transfer in the complete budgeting example in Chapter 12. Here is the scenario. It is the beginning of October, and the hypothetical family is reviewing its budget. Doing some quick calculations, they begin to realize that their Natural Gas Monitored Account is a little low going into the high heating bill months of the winter. After all, they started their budget in August, and hence did not have the advantage of "saving up" for home heating all through the summer.

Transfer between two Monitored Budget Accounts. Certainly, the family has the option of simply paying any overages from their "$" Account. But to make sure the money stays around and to avoid the temptation of spending, they decide to transfer $50 now from the "$" Account to the Natural Gas Monitored Account.

This action is very straightforward. The first step is to "withdraw" fifty dollars from the "$" Account, as shown in Figure 52.

Date	Description	Amount		Balance	
9/15	Payroll	+168	90	551	24
9/16	#434 Bank Card	−128	68	422	56
9/23	#436 Gasoline Refund!	+7	30	429	86
9/29	Payroll—Triple!!!	+1136	15	1566	01
9/30	#439 Stereo	−505	41	1060	60
10/9	Transfer to Natural Gas	−50	00	1010	60

Figure 52: A "$" Account Showing a Transfer to a Natural Gas Monitored Account

Then, the $50 is simply added into the Natural Gas account:

Date	Description	Amount		Balance	
8/16	#423, Bill Under Budget	+22	17	22	17
9/11	—Reconcile—				
9/16	#433, Bill Under Budget	+33	99	56	16
10/9	Transfer from $ Account	+50	00	106	16

Figure 53: A Natural Gas Monitored Account that has just Received a Transfer from a "$" Account

Notice how in both account entries, the family has left a note in the description column explaining the transfer.

Another common use for transfers is to get extra money into your "$" Account. Sometimes, it will happen that you will over budget for utility bills, and a surplus will remain in a monitored account at the end of the year, heating season, or other checkpoint. This is great! Transfer the extra to your "$" Account.

Transfers from a Master Budget Sheet. You can even transfer funds from a Master Budget Sheet to one of your other accounts. An apartment in our area gives a month's free rent to any resident who finds a new renter to fill a vacancy. If one of those residents was using the BudgetYes system, they could place a date in the appropriate "Rent" cell of their Master Budget Sheet, and transfer that full amount to their "$" Account.

Save Old Budget Sheets

 TIP: When you do change your budget and "retire" a Master Budget Sheet, file it away (perhaps with your tax records) for future reference. The old sheets provide a fascinating and valuable record of your expenditures, and can be helpful for planning future budgets, at tax time, or for seeing your financial growth over the years. Don't forget, too, the cross-reference index you have created for every check in your checkbook!

Automatic Adjustments: Raises and Bonuses

This is just a reminder that raises and bonuses are handled *automatically* by the BudgetYes system—no special action on your part is necessary. If you receive a raise, the extra money will automatically land in the "$" Account—exactly where you want it—after you subtract off the monthly expenses reserved on your Master Budget Sheet. Similarly, bonuses can be deposited directly into the "$" Account. In both cases, your discretionary spending money will increase.

Of course, you might *want* to make a budget adjustment when you get a raise. The extra money might make it possible to buy that new car, move to a new home, or increase your savings. Then, by all means, revise your budget to be in alignment with your new goals. But, you do not *have* to do anything—your existing budget will run just fine.

The Magnificent Triple

A few times earlier in this book, we have alluded to a circumstance that is worth discussing in detail. On the surface, it may appear to be something that requires a special budget adjustment or complex accommodations. In reality, your budget system can automatically turn it into something *wonderful*.

This phenomenon occurs if you are paid every other week, for example, every other Friday or every other Wednesday. For most months, you will receive two paychecks. But because of the unequal number of days in each month, and the uneven distribution of weeks across month boundaries, there will be at least two, and very occasionally three, months every year wherein you receive three paychecks instead of two.[6] A third pay of the month is called a "triple" or "triple pay", and can be an awesome windfall to your personal finances.

---

[6] To explain this another way, since there are 52 weeks in the year, and if you are paid every other week, you will receive 26 pays. Distribute these 26 pays over the 12 months, then, and two months will end up with an extra payday.

> If you are paid every other week (26 pays per
> year), then two or three times a year, you will
> receive a third pay in one month, *The Magnificent
> Triple*! Basing your budget on two pays per month
> means two or three times a year you will have a
> whole paycheck to do with as you please!

 TIP: The key to taking advantage of a triple is to always budget as though you are only going to receive two pays per month. In effect, you ignore the triple pays completely during your budget planning. And ignoring the triples completely is easy, since for ten months out of the year you will be limited to just two paychecks.

When a triple occurs, *you get to deposit 100% of your paycheck into your "$" Account!* Imagine what you can do when your entire paycheck is all for you!

The hypothetical family we have been following has triples, and you can see one back in the complete budgeting example presented in Chapter 12. (The triple occurred on September 29th.) In this example, the family got an immediate boost of $1136.15 to their "$" Account. Wow.

NOTE: Triple pays will sometimes be larger than normal pays, because employers often do exactly what we are recommending here and budget for 24 pays instead of 26. As a result, certain taxes and deductions are not withheld from triples. In this case, you get the extra thrill of having the two largest pays of the year be 100% for you!

If you are paid every other week, we heartily recommend that you budget to take advantage of these magnificent triples.

Summary

The BudgetYes system is very easy to modify. Depending on what you need, you can either make a minor adjustment or revise your budget more extensively. Either way, the transitions to these changes are quite simple.

The two most fun adjustments happen automatically. Any increase in pay or bonus you receive goes directly into your "$" Account. And if you are paid biweekly, you will benefit from the Magnificent Triple two or three times a year!

15

Your Money Habits

The way you use, control, and interact with your money is as individual and unique as you are. All of us face different challenges and opportunities every day, have different needs regarding our spending patterns, and handle our funds in different ways.

For simplicity, most of the examples presented in this book so far involve writing checks. But the BudgetYes system is not limited to your checkbook, and it does not require you to use checks to pay for everything. This chapter discusses further methods to customize your personal BudgetYes system to make it fit your needs and payment styles.

Using Cash

Good ol' currency is still one of the most widely used methods for making payments and purchases. And you can tailor your budget to make cash available for whatever purposes you choose to use it.

Idea #1: One common desire or need is to simply have spending money to carry around in pocket, purse, or wallet. This is easy to account for as far as your budget is concerned. Withdraw the money from the bank (from your checkbook) as you usually do—by writing yourself a check, visiting an automated teller machine, completing a withdrawal slip, or whatever method you use. Then deduct the amount from your "$" Account.

Idea #2: Another idea is to use an entry on a Master Budget Sheet to give yourself some pocket money. Suppose, for every Income Event, you wanted to make sure you got $50 in cash for your wallet. You could put an entry titled something like "Spending Money (Cash)" on each Master Budget Sheet, withdraw the money, and then mark the appropriate cell.

Idea #3: Still another technique is to grab some funds for yourself before your budget even knows about it. Let's say that you are paid in cash, and normally deposit the money in your bank. Every payday, you could decide to keep a certain amount for spending money, and deposit the remainder. The amount you deposit, then, would be the amount of your Income Event.

Now, when you put that money in your wallet, can you use it for anything you want to? For example, if you have several dollars with you and stop at the supermarket for a simple purchase such as a loaf a bread, can you just pay cash, or do you have to worry about your Grocery Monitored Account sitting at home in your desk drawer?

The choice is entirely up to you. You can run your budget as tightly or loosely as you wish, depending on your need for control and your personal preferences.

Using the example of the loaf of bread cited above, for many people the easiest thing will be to just pay cash. Often, such a simple transaction for such a small amount will not be worth the bother of a budget entry. But for others who want to impose more discipline on themselves, or to track all of their expenditures very closely, the effort to pull out the checkbook, and later make the appropriate Grocery Monitored Account entry, will be beneficial.

But suppose that you prefer to pay for *all* your groceries using cash rather than a check. Then what?

Idea #4: Remember the classic "envelope method" budgeting system described back in Chapter 2? Combining that technique with BudgetYes will give you a brand new system that incorporates the benefits of both.

By keeping a dedicated envelope in your wallet or purse containing money specifically earmarked for your groceries, you can pay in cash and still retain the benefits of the control of a personal budget. You can "load" the envelope using any of the methods described earlier—withdrawing funds from a Monitored Budget Account, reserving money via a Master Budget Sheet, or keeping money out before you deposit your pay.

Of course, you can carry around as many envelopes as you are comfortable with—groceries, gasoline, entertainment, and "eating out" are common ones. Of course, you don't have to use envelopes. Special wallet or purse compartments and little multi-chambered coin purses can accomplish the same thing. To separate bills for different purposes in your wallet, you can use paper clips, rubber bands, or little cardboard or heavy paper dividers.

Idea #5: One other technique for using cash is to adjust your budget after the fact to reflect how the cash was actually used. Let's say you withdrew $50 from your "$" Account, intending to use it as "mad money." Then, learning of some unexpected guests for dinner and being caught without your checkbook, you end up spending $30 of the $50 at the local market on your way home from work. You could adjust your budget by transferring $30 from your Grocery Monitored Account to your "$" Account, and everything would be in synch again. We will discuss more details on how to make such transfers shortly.

Using Credit Cards

Typically, consensus would indicate that budgets and credit cards are strange bedfellows. This is generally true because the cards have no automatic governors or controls, and can lead to unchecked purchases and impulse buying.

Correctly used, however, credit cards can be wonderful financial management tools. They provide detailed records in the form of monthly statements. They allow you to defer your payments for some time after a purchase, giving your money the opportunity to continue working for you after it is spent. Some cards even give bonuses each time you use them such as cash back, credits toward the purchase of automobiles, points toward free airline tickets, or donations to targeted institutions.

Important Point about Credit Card Usage

Pay cards off completely every month. If you do not pay your charge bills in their entirety, the credit card interest you pay will be an enormous setback to your budget. Paying credit card interest—even for the lowest interest rates—is like having an enormous leak in your checkbook, allowing your hard-earned money to disappear with nothing to show for it.

> The **key** to benefiting from credit card use is to *pay off the entire balance*, every month!

If, and only if, you are disciplined enough to pay off your credit card balances routinely, an occasional month or two of paying some small amount of interest is nothing to be concerned about, and might even be a smart move if done for the right reason. This could happen, for example, if a big ticket item you have been eyeing suddenly goes on sale, but you do not quite have the full amount of the purchase price saved up. Covering the balance with your credit card would be a wise financial move if the interest you pay for a month or two is less than the amount you saved by taking advantage of the sale. If the sale price was $300 off, and you end up paying around $100 interest over the next two months until your credit card balance is back to zero, you are still $200 ahead. This kind of opportunity is an even better bet if you had a Master Budget Sheet item set up to save for the big ticket expense—the budgeted item will help guarantee you can pay off the credit card balance quickly.

There are other reasonable situations where incurring some credit card debt makes sense. A family emergency, for example, is certainly a case where a line of plastic credit can help you make ends meet for awhile.

☑ **NOTE:** If you are routinely making the minimum payment on your credit card bills every month, or have run the cards up to the maximum and are keeping them there, your top priority should be to get those balances down to zero. Set up a Monitored Budget Item to pay off your cards as quickly as you can (start with the card charging you the biggest interest rate). Decide on the highest amount you can afford to pay every month, and budget that amount on your Master Budget Sheet. It will be enormously satisfying to watch yourself chip away at the balance month after month. And when you finally achieve your goal, you will be able to use the money you were formerly paying in interest to increase your own financial strength, instead of increasing the profits of some banking conglomerate.

While you are paying off your balance, do not make the problem worse by using your cards to incur any more debt. Lock them away. Give them to a trusted friend. Cut them in half if you have to.[7] Once your balance is zero, you can begin using them again—wisely this time—with the proviso of a commitment to pay the balance in full every month.

The BudgetYes system can be a valuable tool to make sure your credit card bills are covered every month. By setting up amounts for expenditures, and then tracking your spending closely with Master Budget Sheets and Monitored Budget Accounts, you can guarantee you will have the money for that next bill.

---

[7] While cutting cards in half has almost become the knee-jerk conventional wisdom for solving credit card debt, it can open you to vulnerabilities in times of emergency. Financial institutions can require many days to issue replacement cards, and in a situation such as a medical emergency, you may not have the luxury of being able to wait. Trusting a relative, friend, or other responsible party to keep your cards is probably your best bet: the other person can help approve your decision that the plastic cards need to be dragged out to deal with an urgent circumstance.

What to Look for in a Credit Card

Since you should not be using credit cards to maintain consumer debt, but just as a convenience, *then once you have your cards paid off*, the interest rate of the card is not of great importance. The only credit cards you should consider are those that require no annual fee and have a grace period of at least 30 days. Finding cards that also offer benefits, such as free gas, groceries, or discounts on vehicles is a bonus!

How to Handle Credit Card Purchases

What if you use bank cards to pay for more than one type of budgeted item? In a typical day, you might use plastic to pay for groceries, gasoline, clothes, and even a utility bill or two—all of which are different items within your budget. How do you "tell" your budget what has been spent for what?

There are three different accounting techniques for handling credit card purchases within the BudgetYes system. You can use whichever methods appeal to you, or be imaginative and create some customized combination of the techniques.

Post-process your bank card statement. With this approach, you use your cards throughout the month exactly as you do now, without doing anything special. Then, when the monthly bank card statement arrives, you look over the expenditures and decide which charges apply to your various budget items. You then make the appropriate deductions within your budget, just as if you were paying a number of separate bills.

One way to accomplish the segregation of the various items on your bank card statement is to use a set of colored highlighting markers. Take a green highlighter, for example, and mark all of

the grocery expenditures. Then mark all of the gasoline purchases in yellow. Clothing purchases could be pink, and so on.
When all the items have been categorized, total the amounts corresponding to each color, and deduct each total from the appropriate location within your budget. Any leftover amount that is
not categorized should be deducted from the "$" Account. The
subtotals for each color, and whatever amount you deduct from
the "$" Account, should sum to the total amount of the bank
card bill.

Using this procedure, the number of the check that you use to
pay your bank card bill will likely appear in several places
throughout your budget. The number may be entered in several
Master Budget Sheet cells, next to Monitored Budget Account
entries, and on the "$" Account. The sum of all the entries will
be the total amount of the check. Hence, you will have effectively distributed a single payment across many different items of
your budget.

Use multiple credit cards. In today's world, bank cards are very
easy to obtain. If your household is like most, you probably
receive new offers for additional credit cards on a weekly basis!
To reiterate the conventional wisdom, owning many cards is
usually unwise because of the temptation they offer of going into
debt. However, if you are under the discipline of a budget, and
faithfully pay 100% of all your bills every month, then having
multiple cards can be advantageous.

If there are several major budgeting categories you routinely use
credit cards to pay for—for example, groceries, gasoline, clothing,
or eating out—consider using a separate card for each. Hence,
you would have a collection of cards in your wallet or purse, and
would always use one of them for all your grocery purchases,
another for all your gasoline purchases, etcetera.

Doing things this way provides you with a separate, detailed statement each month for all of your expenditures for each item. It is easy, then, to pay each bill from the appropriate Master Budget Sheet item or Monitored Budget Account.

NOTE: If you run a small business, using a separate credit card for all your expenses related to the business is practically a necessity. You will need the segregated statements and accounts for deductions at tax time.

There is another benefit that may apply. Earlier, we discussed how some cards give you premiums or bonuses, such as vacations or cash back, when you use them. Sometimes, however, there is a catch. We have a card issued by our grocery store that is valid anywhere. We can use it to buy gasoline, go to the movies, or pay for a hotel room. However, it only pays us bonuses—in this case, credit toward free groceries—when we use it at the store where it was issued. Similarly, another card issued by the gasoline station down the street gives credit when used to buy gas, but not for other purchases.

TIP: Using multiple cards for specific purposes can help you play these games to your advantage. For example, make the card you use for grocery purchases be the one that pays you bonuses for buying groceries. You will maximize the benefits you receive from each card's bonus program. Also, as mentioned above, only select cards that require no annual fee and have a grace period of at least 30 days.

Use a Monitored Budget Account. This technique provides the greatest feedback and control for credit card purchases, because it allows your budget to process each expenditure as it occurs. *This is especially necessary for those on very tight budgets.*

The key to this method is to set up a Monitored Budget Account specifically for the purpose of paying your next bank card bill. If you want a long, descriptive title for this account, you could use something like "A Monitored Budget Account to Accumulate Funds to Pay the Next Bank Card Bill." ☺ A shorter title might be "Bank Card Payment." The account would start with a zero balance.

Usually, when you pay by credit card, you sign a receipt, and get a copy of that receipt to take home. In this technique, you treat those receipts as if they were bills.

Suppose you go to the grocery store and spend $123.46. You would then take the receipt home and deduct that amount from your Grocery Monitored Account. Then, add $123.46 into your new "Bank Card Payment" account. You have effectively transferred the $123.46 from one account to another.

Next, suppose you use your card for an expense that would normally come out of your "$" Account. When you get home, transfer the amount on your receipt from the "$" Account to the "Bank Card Payment" account. You can do the same thing for Master Budget Sheet items—just put a date in the appropriate cell and add the corresponding amount into the bank card Monitored Budget Account.

Allowing that all of your bank card expenditures are received and processed by the financial institution in time, when your bill comes, your "Bank Card Payment" account will contain the *exact* amount you need to pay the bill in full! If not all of the transactions clear, the extra money will stay in the Monitored Budget Account until the next bill comes. At any rate, using this method, you can be guaranteed that you will always pay off your bank card bill in full.

This technique can help you stay within your self-imposed spending limits, because as you deduct each expense from the appropriate area, your budget will show you how much you have left in that category.

Overlaying Investment Accounts

The BudgetYes system is not limited to overlaying just checking accounts. You can set up separate overlays for any account you desire: your savings account, mutual funds, retirement funds—anything.

There are many situations where an overlay of another account might be helpful to you. Here is one example. Suppose that you have found a savings vehicle that you are quite happy with. It is paying you a good interest rate, allows you convenient access, and you are delighted with the service you receive. As a result, you are using that single account to save up for a number of things: your next vacation, a new car, holiday gifts at the end of the year, and some new furniture.

An overlay of this account would show you how much you had saved for each purpose, and would keep the funds separate even though they are all saved together. To accomplish this, set up one Monitored Budget Account for each item involved. Every time you make a deposit for one of your items, you add the amount to the appropriate Monitored Budget Account. At all times, the totals of all the Monitored Budget Accounts should sum to the amount of money in the account.

Using this idea, you have complete control over what to do with the interest you earn on your savings. When interest is paid, you get to decide which of your sub-categories it is assigned to. You can divide it up equally, assign percentages based on the relative size of the Monitored Budget Account totals, or, if you are on a "fast track" to save up for one item quickly, you can assign all of the interest there.

✓ **NOTE:** Reconciling these types of systems is easy—just make sure that the sum of all the sub-categories (the Monitored Budget Accounts) always sum to the total in the savings vehicle.

On the subject of investment accounts, we should suggest that if you find yourself dealing with large amounts of money in your checkbook, you might consider moving those funds out to other financial vehicles where your money will work harder for you and give you a better return. The fact that your checkbook is earning interest for you is important, and it is a good account for the routine bills and expenses you are faced with. But checking accounts do not provide the kinds of returns that other financial instruments are capable of.

Some people using the BudgetYes system are surprised at how rapidly extra money can accumulate in their "$" Account (and we *sincerely* hope this happens to you!). Others might be saving for big ticket items such as a down payment for a house or a new car. If you find yourself in one or more of these situations, where the accumulation of thousands of dollars is not unlikely, by all means explore your options of a more lucrative investment, and move the money out of your checking account.

It is possible to have one BudgetYes system overlay multiple financial accounts. Still anchoring the system on your checkbook, you can treat other savings vehicles as auxiliary Monitored Budget Accounts. For example, if on your Master Budget Sheet you have an item that is saving for a house down payment, when you "move" that money to its Monitored Budget Account, what you would actually do is transfer the amount from your checkbook to the alternate savings vehicle. If this idea of a "master" BudgetYes system appeals to you, go for it!

Income Event Normalization

In Chapter 4, where we introduced the concept of Income Events, we mentioned that the BudgetYes system itself can do the "normalization" necessary for irregular incomes. (To review, the normalization is necessary if you are paid more than four times a month, such as a waitress or waiter who receives tips every day, or less than twelve times a year, such as a teacher who chooses to take the summer off.) The trick to this internal normalization is to use a Monitored Budget Account, and then move money back and forth from that account as necessary.

Suppose, for example, that you receive a large portion of your income in tips, and the tips come in every day you work. But you want it to look to your budget as if you are paid once a month, so that you can have just one Master Budget Sheet. To do this, set up a Monitored Budget Account named something like "Tip Income" or just "Income". Then, whenever you deposit your tips into your checking account, add the amount of the deposit to the "Income" account.

When it is time for your monthly Income Event (whenever you decide it should be), deduct the total shown at the bottom of your Master Budget Sheet from the "Income" account, and enter the date at the top of the next empty column on the Master Budget Sheet. The money has been "transferred" so that you can use it to cover all your monthly budget items! At the same time, you may also move some money from the "Income" account to the "$" Account.

If you wish, you can simplify things by using the "$" Account as your "Income" account. Deposit all your income into the "$" Account, and then, once or twice a month, whatever you choose, move money over to your Master Budget Sheet.

Of course, you can sidestep as much of the depositing process as you like. If you want to keep some spending money in your wallet, you can just put it there, and then deposit the rest. You do not have to go through the trouble of putting it in your checkbook and then withdrawing it. Similarly, if you are using a modified version of the envelope method to pay cash for certain expenditures, you can "load" your funds directly from the cash you take in, without having to go through the bother of the accounting in your budget. For example, twice a month you might take $45.00 of your tip money and set it aside in a special place, reserving it to be used for the purchase of gasoline.

The same technique works if you are paid less than 12 times per year, such as seasonal workers, salespersons who receive periodic large commissions, or businesses that take in the majority of their income during certain periods. Deposit your funds into a Monitored Budget Account, and then move a sum every month to cover the expenses of the Master Budget Sheet. As a reminder, it is probable that if you are in one of these situations, large amounts of money may well be involved. It will be in your interest to find a more lucrative account than your checkbook to hold the balance between your Income Events.

Summary

Whatever your money habits are, you can use BudgetYes to help you where you need it. If you want to deal primarily with cash so you are not tempted with credit cards, there are many ways to do this. If you have the discipline to use credit cards to your advantage without carrying any debt, do it. If you need closer controls on your income or spending, or a debt repayment plan, the Monitored Account is your answer.

16

Budgeting on a Computer

If you have a computer in your home, a natural question is whether you can or should run your budget via software programs. There are many alternatives available to accomplish this, and if you are comfortable using your computer, we encourage you to investigate some.

Seven Advantages of Computers

No more arithmetic! There are many advantages to using a computer for budgeting. The biggest, perhaps, is that you will never have to do arithmetic again! The software becomes responsible for all the addition, subtraction, and balancing. Reconciling—both within your budget and with your bank statement—becomes much, much easier and faster.

This is not to say that mistakes will not happen. There is still the possibility for error: a wrong amount will be keyed in, a transaction might be forgotten and not entered at all. But with the computer responsible for all the computations, the chances for error are significantly reduced, and the mistakes you do make will be much easier to find.

Every item is "monitored". Another advantage of computers is that you can effectively treat every budgeted item as a Monitored Budget Item. Using a paper system, ten or fifteen Monitored Budget Accounts can be unwieldy. But the computer doesn't care how many logical accounts it has to keep track of. Added monitoring will give you more information and more control.

Less effort. Tying in with the previous advantage is the ability to budget for more items with less effort. While on paper you might only be comfortable with the work associated with ten or so budget items, the computer can handle as many categories as you care to throw at it. Again, the more budgeted items, the more information and control you will have regarding your expenditures.

Analysis of your money. Computers can also provide you more information about your money by performing analysis of your financial data. Charts, graphs, and reports can show you patterns and predict trends. Automatic reminders can be set up to help you pay your bills on time. And your income and expenses can automatically be sorted and categorized at tax time.

Pay bills online. Some computer software provides the ability to pay bills online through a modem. This convenience eliminates writing checks, stamping envelopes, and putting things in the mail. Electronic payments also let you make your monetary outlays in a more timely fashion: since the transactions happen instantaneously, you no longer have to make payments a week or two in advance to allow for postal delivery times. This, in turn, lets you keep your money longer.

Manage investments. Some personal finance programs do much more than simply balance your checkbook and run your budget. They can manage your total financial picture, including investments, loans, savings, and retirement planning. They have the ability to do complex interest calculations and help plan or restructure mortgages. Some even provide investment advice, dynamically make suggestions as to how to improve your overall fiscal position, and contain tutorials and interactive learning forums for sharpening your financial acumen. In short, this type of software can be your link to control and understanding of your complete financial picture.

More fun! Finally, many people will find that running a computerized budget just makes the whole process more fun. Software packages often have colorful graphics, animation, and even sound effects as part of the user interface, all of which can combine to make bill paying a lot more pleasant.

Commercial Software

There are several commercial software packages on the market that manage your budget and finances. You should find it easy to transition to one of these programs, because all of the basic concepts you have learned in the BudgetYes system are fundamental ideas shared by all good budgeting systems.

The program will have areas to enter monthly budget amounts for budgeted items, taking the place of the Master Budget Sheets. The assignment of expense categories when you pay a check will provide you the same functionality as Monitored Budget Accounts. And having the program report on your unbudgeted funds, or assigning a special expense category for your spending money, will be the reincarnation of your friend the "$" Account in computerized form.

Difference Between Software and BudgetYes

Despite the similarities, there is one major difference that should be highlighted when you move from paper to computer. The distinction is subtle but very important.

As you have seen, the emphasis of the BudgetYes is one of planning and looking forward. The system enables you to decide up front how you want to allocate and spend your money, and then provides tools and controls that allow you stick to your plan and monitor your progress.

✓ **NOTE:** The paradigm behind the major software programs is just the opposite. There, the software asks you to record your transactions, and afterwards, takes a retrospective view to tell you how you did.

Certainly, this retrospective view is valuable, and was cited in the advantages listed above. Early in our first chapter we recalled that "knowledge is power," and knowing what went on over the past week, month, or year in your checkbook will give you insights and information to make informed decisions in the future. However, the charts, graphs, and reports can lull you into a false sense of security, making you believe that you are following a budget when all you are doing is carefully documenting your existing spending patterns. To take this to the extreme, it would be possible (and easy!) for a person to be wildly overspending, enter all the expenditures in her or his handy budget program, and then announce to friends and family: "Oh, everything's fine—after all, I *am* on a budget!"

Now that you have learned the BudgetYes system, you have a big advantage that will allow you to use computer programs to control as well as track. The secret is just a shift in thinking.

How to Handle the Difference

With BudgetYes, every time you spend some money you have the opportunity and ability to decide how to handle the expense. If you are over budget, you must decide how to accommodate the excess. If you are under budget, you get to decide what to do with the extra funds.

So do the same thing when using your computer. Rather than writing a check, and then telling the software, "Oh, by the way, here's what I did," go to the program *first* and look at the impacts of the check you are about to write. Are you over budget? If so, why? And if so, where is the extra money going to come from? What changes can you or should you make to prevent a similar problem in the future? Now, you are in *control*. Write your check and enter your transactions appropriately. You will be leveraging the power of your record-keeping to the fullest.

If you are thinking of switching to a computer-based budgeting system, you might find it to be a useful exercise to run the BudgetYes system in its paper form for several months first. The good habits you will acquire can form a mindset that you will value for the rest of your life.

Creating Your Own System

One of the foundation principles of BudgetYes is customizability—allowing you to tailor your budgeting system and practices to your needs, goals, and habits. If you are versed in computer spreadsheet or database packages, you might want to have a try at creating your own computerized system.

Spreadsheets and BudgetYes go hand in hand. With spreadsheets, you can enter data, sum columns of numbers, and perform computations and cross-checks between different values. As a start, you might set up spreadsheets for all of your Monitored Budget Accounts, including your "$" Account, to keep running tallies of balances. Then you could extend that one step further by creating a spreadsheet to act as your checkbook register. The ambitious could even simulate a Master Budget Sheet, making automatic deductions, showing balances, and transferring funds in and out of the other worksheets.

Database programs give you even more flexibility. You can design custom data entry screens for income and expenditures, with check boxes or selection boxes indicating how each amount should be distributed. Reports can then be designed to automatically show balances in your checkbook, Monitored Budget Accounts, and for each budget item.

Summary

Commercial financial management software programs provide a retrospective on your finances, they *track* your money, whereas BudgetYes *controls* your money by planning and looking forward. Even so, there are many terrific advantages to budgeting on a computer, but you must keep the philosophical difference in mind. If you have never run a budget, and would like to use a computer, you'll probably find it valuable to run BudgetYes manually with paper and calculator for 3 to 6 months first. The good habits you learn will help you better understand what the computer is doing, and *not* doing, for you.

17

Where Do You Go From Here?

You now have all the information you need to set up and run the BudgetYes system for yourself and begin reaping the benefits of budgeting and control over your finances.

But now what? Once you have mastered your own budget, and running it has become second nature, what is the next step?

A budget can be your passport into a larger, exciting world of opportunities for financial growth and security. Once you have a solid budget as a foundation, the sky is the limit for new avenues to explore and from which to take advantage.

Following are some suggestions for some places to start. These are things that have worked wonders for us or those we respect, and we pass them along in hope they will benefit you as well. But these are only a few starting points. Your imagination, drive, and dreams will lead you to discoveries throughout your life. Keep building, learning, and never stop asking "what's next?"

Written Goals

There is an old truism that if you do not know where you are going, you will never know when you have arrived.

Goals allow us to focus our attention, our energies, and even the processes of our subconscious minds. They allow us to set our priorities. Goals can even be a communication tool to those important to us as we seek help, and as we offer our help to others.

Did you ever notice that when you begin concentrating on something, information and resources begin appearing out of thin air? Let's say you are in the market for a new car. Suddenly, you begin to notice all the new cars out on the road. You overhear a conversation at work, and find out a close friend has just purchased one of the new models you are considering. You open the paper and find an article with tips for new car buyers. Your bank sends you a flier listing attractive interest rates for new car loans.

These events are more than happenstance or coincidence. The point is, the cars, the conversations, the newspaper articles and the junk mail are always there, along with an uncountable number of other information inputs that your senses receive every day. You filter out what doesn't interest you, and focus on the data that you need. Your goals are your focus controls.

The better and more focused your goals, the more quickly and efficiently will the puzzle pieces arrive and fall into place.

All of us have dreams. We talk about the new car that would be nice to have, the new career we would like to pursue, the people we would like to help, the early retirement we would like to enjoy, the vacation we would like to take "someday."

The difference between a dream and a goal is that a goal is written down.

The focusing energy that written goals provide is amazing. There is something magical about putting ink on paper. Seeing something in black and white makes it official and establishes a commitment.

There is one practice that is essential when creating written goals (besides the obvious one that they must be *written*): they *must* be detailed and specific. Don't simply write "new car." Put the make and model. The color. The accessories. The price. And the date you will pick it up. Don't simply write "vacation." Put the destination. The date you will leave and the date you will return. The name of the hotel, campground, or other accommodations where you want to stay. And details of what you want to do while you are gone.

A popular acronym to remember this method is called the SMART model, shown in Figure 54.

SMART Model	
S	pecific
M	easurable
A	chievable
R	esults-Oriented
T	ime-Bound

Figure 54: SMART Model for Goal Setting

With your written goals in hand, get your budget to reflect them. Say your goal is to buy a new car. If the goal is specific, as it should be, you know the amount you need. You also know the date of the purchase, and hence know how long you have. A few arithmetic calculations will show you how much you have to save every month to achieve your goal. Set up an item on your Master Budget Sheet, and watch your goal being reached. If your goal is to be debt free by a certain date, similar calculations will show you how much of your balances have to be paid off every month. Your goals and your budget will provide a wonderful synergy.

One other practice that is useful involving goals is to review them. First, review them with others they affect—your family, significant others, work teams, business associates—to make sure everyone is on the same wavelength and all pushing in the same direction. Secondly, review them yourself frequently—daily if possible. There will be course corrections, and your goals will change. But keeping focused will allow you to constantly apply your best energies, and your finances, in the most profitable direction.

Take Advantage of Money Management Tips

There are many excellent suggestions and strategies in books, periodicals, financial reports, newspaper articles, and even computer software, that offer tips and techniques for managing your money wisely. These suggestions involve things such as reducing auto insurance costs by eliminating unnecessary premiums, creatively restructuring mortgage payments to pay less interest, maximizing tax deductions, adjusting life insurance policies to work better for you, and wise investment strategies.

The frustration most people face when trying to take advantage of such tips is that often their saved money never shows up anywhere. If they save $200 a year on their car insurance, they do not end up with an extra $200 in their pockets—the extra money is sucked up by circumstances that seem beyond their control. So there is little incentive to even pursue the savings in the first place!

With the BudgetYes system's "$" Account working for you, however, you *will* see savings that you successfully implement. If you save $200 on a payment, that extra $200 will move to your "$" Account and be available for you to use as you see fit. Make it an objective to always be on the lookout for ways to grow your favorite account. Even little things like coupons, rebates, and sale items will add together, and, over time, you should see a steady growth in the amount of discretionary money you have.

See the "Personal Finance" section at your library or bookstore for information on smart money handling.

Plan for Retirement

Retirement planning is usually one of the first topics that comes to mind when people start thinking about their budgets and financial future. The key to investing for your retirement years is to start as early in life as you can. The earlier you begin, the more the compounding and re-compounding of interest will add to your personal nest egg.

To illustrate the power of compound interest, let's compare a hypothetical example of two savers—one who starts the process early, and the other who waits awhile before thinking about retirement.

The first person begins saving at age 21. She invests $100 every month for only ten years, and stops the process on her 31st birthday. At that point, her total investment is $12,000, and she lets it sit, earning interest, until retirement at age 65.

The second person waits until age 35 to begin saving for retirement. She still puts away $100 every month, but *continues* to do so up until age 65. So her total investment is $36,000. Like the first person, she never touches a penny of the investment until her retirement.

So who ends up with more money? Intuition might say that the second person, who invested more ($36,000 instead of $12,000) would end up ahead. But the earlier investor has time and compound interest on her side. Assuming an annual return of 8%, compounded monthly, the first investor would end up with $300,053, while the second would only have $150,030. In other words, the first person would invest $24,000 less than the second, but would end up with $150,023 more!

This phenomenon is shown graphically in Figure 55.

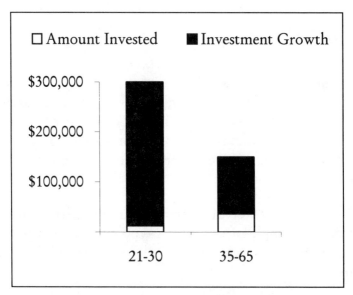

Figure 55: A Comparison of Different Retirement Investment Strategies

Let's look at a few more examples to drive this point home. Suppose that the first person, instead of stopping their investment at age 31, had continued investing $100 every month until retirement at age 65? There, her total investment of $52,800 would result in a nest egg of nearly a half million dollars: $489,120!

Now, take the example to the extreme. Let's pretend you just had a new baby, and wanted to ensure a golden retirement for her or him. When baby is born, you begin depositing $100 every month into an investment account. You continue to do that until the child's 6th birthday, at which point you stop. You leave the money in the account and never touch it. Again assuming the 8% interest rate, when the child retires at age 65, your investment of $7,200 would have grown to over a million dollars—$1,107,869!

Naturally, these are hypothetical examples and the results of your own investments may earn more or less than the amounts given. Also, taxes will have to be paid either on the interest as it is earned, or, if the investments are in a tax-deferred account, when the money is withdrawn. Those facts notwithstanding, the point is still worth noting. Starting today is better than starting tomorrow. Starting this week is better than starting next.

Aside from starting early, another major variable in the retirement savings process is the amount you save every month. Obviously, the more you put away, the larger your savings, and the faster your investment will grow.

With a carefully constructed budget, you will have an excellent understanding of your monthly income and expenditures. That knowledge will translate directly into how much you can afford for your retirement savings. Meet with a financial or investment analyst, or the Personnel or Compensation office at your place of employment, and begin your program. Make the savings a permanent part of your budget. Years from now, you will be *so* glad you did!

Three Benefits of Automatic Payments

Several times throughout this book, we have mentioned the concept of automatic payments. As the name implies, these allow your bills to be paid automatically, by computer transfer, without the need for any work or intervention on your part.

For the average person who is not running a budget, using automatic payments is a terrifying thought. The idea that a computer can come along and suddenly deduct money from their checking account seems to invite financial problems and loss of control over their money.

But with the BudgetYes system, you are always in control. If you have arranged to take care of a bill via automatic payment, then by budgeting for that item via the Master Budget Sheet, you can *guarantee* the money will be there when the computer goes to deduct it.

Saves time. So why use automatic payments? There are tremendous advantages. Time savings is one of the biggest and probably most obvious benefits. When your bills are paid by computer, you no longer have to spend time writing checks, licking envelopes, and getting things in the mail.

Speaking of mail, postage savings can add up. With today's postal rates, for every three bills you do not have to mail, you save around a dollar.

No late payments. Another convenience is peace of mind that your bills will always be paid on time. Being away from home for a vacation or business trip can cause grief in the bill paying department. A busy or commotion-filled week can cause payment deadlines to slip by without being noticed. But with computers paying your bills for you, you will never again miss another due date. And *you* will get the reputation for having an excellent credit record!

Extra money. Finally, the use of automatic payments may actually improve your cash flow. For once, your creditor's computers are on your side and act like "nice guys." The automatic payments are generally set up to withdraw the funds from your account at the last possible moment. This leaves the money in your hands longer, earning interest.

Automatic payments can be set up with utility companies, through your bank, or via special service providers. Generally, all you have to do is sign an authorization form, and send in a copy of a voided check or deposit slip. Then, a week or two before the money is withdrawn, you will receive a confirmation statement showing the date that the payment will be made, and the amount. The statement will also list a telephone number for you to call if there are questions or problems. Then, on the indicated date, the payment is taken care of for you. The transaction will show up as an entry on your next checking account statement.

If you are new to automatic payments, consider setting up just one—perhaps with a local utility company—to see how convenient they are. Then, once you are comfortable with the process, expand to other utilities, house payments or rent, savings, investments, and retirement plans. Don't be surprised if you get "hooked" and soon have much of your budget on autopilot!

Pay Yourself After Repaying Loans

A common budget item is the repayment of a loan. With your goals in mind and the discipline of your budget in place, the day will come when you make the final payment on your car, credit card balance, student loan, bill consolidation program, or even your mortgage.

 TIP: At that point, consider continuing the loan payments—but pay *yourself* instead of your creditor. The point is, you will be in the habit of making the payments. Your budget is already set up for the monthly deduction. You didn't "miss" the money you used for payments when you didn't have it to spend. So before you get accustomed to having the extra funds at your disposal, commit to socking the payments away for your personal financial growth.

For example, let's say that you have just paid off your car. Next month, instead of sending the payment off in the mail, put the same amount into a Monitored Budget Account, or, better yet, a savings or money market account. Continuing this practice will eventually provide you with the down payment for your next car. If you challenge yourself and save aggressively, you might even get ahead of the game and be able to pay cash for your next automobile! Doing this can save you thousands upon thousands of dollars, completely eliminating any interest you pay. (Most sellers will give a discount for cash payments, too!) You can then begin the process over for your next car.

Other ideas for paying yourself include the creation of an emergency fund, beginning or adding to retirement savings, college funds, vacations, or home improvements.

This technique of making payments to yourself is a very powerful one for meeting your financial goals. The beauty of it is that after you pay the "bill," you still have the money!

Pay Yourself With Windfalls

Occasionally, it may be your good fortune to be hit with an unexpected windfall, such as a raise, a bonus, or a large gift of money. Paying yourself with this unexpected income can be a painless way to increase your savings.

This tip applies particularly if you are living comfortably within your current budget and are making ends meet within your current lifestyle. Again, before you get used to having the extra money, consider paying yourself first by committing to new or increased savings programs. This is a smart way to build wealth without touching any of your current expenditures.

Use Your Budget for Self-improvement

As we have seen, budgets are tremendous tools for self-improvement. They can get you organized, improve your credit, provide extra income, put you in control of your spending and investing, and improve your total financial picture. In addition, a budget offers many opportunities for you to push yourself in as many directions as you have the desire to pursue.

Have you been meaning to get back to school to improve your skills or even aspire to a new career? Your budget can help you plan for the tuition payments. Have you been thinking about starting a business of your own? Your budget is the tool you need to plan for the capital you will need to start your new venture. How about joining that aerobics class or purchasing exercise equipment for your home? By now, you are an expert at setting up Master Budget Sheet items to make all these dreams come true.

Budgets can help with the "negatives" as well as the "positives." If, for example, there is a habit you are trying to break that is costing you money, try setting up a Monitored Budget Account to track the costs in stark black and white. Sometimes this type of accounting can provide the extra incentive you need to change your behavior. Afterwards, use the money you save to treat yourself to something you really want.

Summary

Writing down your goals, taking advantage of money management tips, planning for your retirement, making use of automatic payments, paying yourself first, and creating new habits, are all part of the sunny horizon beyond your *primary* financial management tool of running a personal budget.

Successes lead to successes. Ride the wave of the achievements you obtain with your budget to pave the way for other accomplishments, and then leverage the new accomplishments to even greater things.

18

Final Thought

You have all the skills. You know all the tricks. The only thing left for you to do is to *try* a budget and see the amazing benefits that you will accrue.

Is there anything magic about a budget? Yes and no.

It is the same kind of magic involved in planting a garden. Everyone knows if you throw some seeds in fertile ground, water them occasionally, and wait a season, they will grow and produce. Science can explain the entire process, and we often take it for granted. But when you sit back and ponder the phenomenon, there is something truly miraculous about it! You pop a tiny seed into the ground, dump some water on it, and, given time, you are soon enjoying juicy tomatoes; crisp, pungent peppers; or delicious sweet corn.

The seeds will grow. The question is whether or not you take the time to plant them.

Most everyone agrees and understands that running a solid budget is a good idea. But not everyone understands just how delicious and sweet the results can be.

> The *real* secret of a budget is that it is a tool to help *you* function better. It is an instrument panel for your finances. The more information you have, the better decisions you will be able to make.

If you don't think feedback is important when you are in control, try driving a car blindfolded! ☺ For an important task such as driving, where lives are at stake, we go to great lengths to get as much information as possible to the driver: mirrors, glass all around, instruments that measure speed and tell how the engine is performing.

Think of what would happen if you were to take just *one* instrument away from the driver. Suppose you were to put a piece of tape over the gas gauge. The person might become stranded, forced to spend time and money to get going again. The alternative is that the driver would stop for gasoline much more frequently than needed, wasting time to ensure that the tank always had an adequate supply.

Running your finances without a budget is like driving blindfolded. But running a loose budget that does not give you enough information is like driving with tape all over your dashboard. The BudgetYes system can accommodate as many controls as you care to throw at it. Each line item on a Master Budget Sheet, and each Monitored Budget Account, is another gauge giving you precious information as to what is going on.

Please give it a try. Plant the seed. Use it for six months, and watch the magic that will happen.

Appendix A

This appendix provides a template that, if assembled and photo-copied, will produce full-sized versions of the Master Budget Sheet format used throughout this book. You can then use the blank forms to make your own Master Budget Sheets.

The Master Budget Sheet is reproduced in this book in two halves, one on each of the following two pages. To assemble the sheet, cut the two halves out of the book on the lines indicated. You may also trim a half-inch strip from the top of each page (a dotted line there acts as a guide); doing this will make the width of the page the standard 8½ inches.

Once the two pages have been cut out, join them together in the middle, along the long cuts that separated the pages from the book. Secure them with a piece of tape or two, and you will have a master than can be placed on the flat bed of a photocopy machine.

If you do not wish to destroy this book, you might consider copying the pages first, and then cutting and pasting the copied pages.

You might notice that the Master Budget Sheet is copyrighted. The purchase of this book gives a license to you and those resid-ing in your household to make unlimited copies of the template for use in setting up and running a budget. Specifically, the sale of this form or the BudgetYes system is expressly prohibited.

Appendix B

This appendix provides a template that, if assembled an
copied, will produce full-sized versions of the Monitore   t
Account format used throughout this book. You can   e
the blank forms to make your own "$" Accounts and N
Budget Accounts.

Like the Master Budget Sheet in Appendix A, the   ed
Budget Account is reproduced in this book in two hal·   on
each of the following two pages. The instructions p   in
Appendix A can be used to assemble this sheet.

The blank line on the top right corner of the Monit   dget
Account form can be used to indicate the name of   ount
for which the sheet will be used, for example, "$" A   Gro-
cery, Entertainment, Clothing, etc.

Like the Master Budget Sheet, the Monitored Bud   unt is
copyrighted. The purchase of this book gives a lice   ɔu and
those residing in your household to make unlimite   of the
template for use in setting up and running a budg   fically,
the sale of this form or the BudgetYes system is e>   prohibited.

BudgetYes

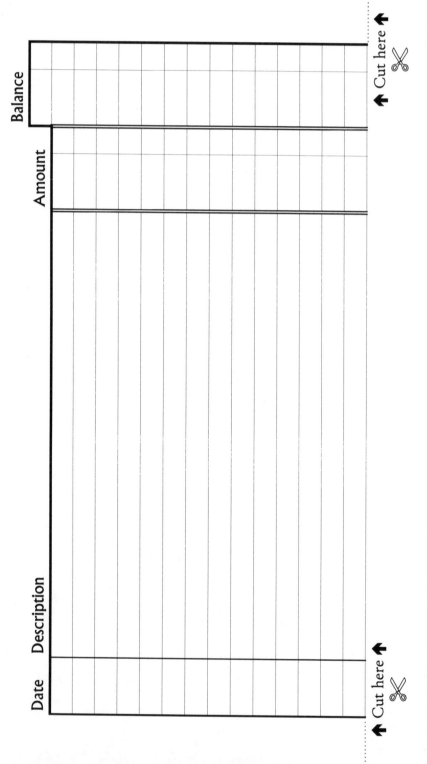

Date	Description	Amount	Balance

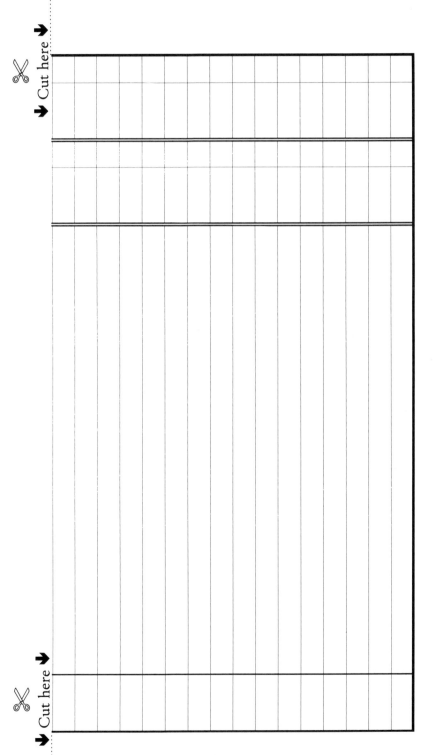

✂ Cut here ➜

➜ Cut here ➜

✂ Cut here ➜

➜

Appendix C

List of Possible Budget Items

- ☐ Accountant Fees
- ☐ Alimony
- ☐ Annuities and IRAs
- ☐ Baby-sitting
- ☐ Benefit Plans
- ☐ Birthday and Holiday Gifts
- ☐ Carpeting and Drapery Cleaning
- ☐ Charge Accounts
- ☐ Charitable Contributions
- ☐ Child Care
- ☐ Child Support
- ☐ Children's Allowances
- ☐ Chiropractic Care
- ☐ Christmas Club
- ☐ Clothing
- ☐ Club or Union Dues
- ☐ Coin Laundry
- ☐ Contributions or Donations
- ☐ Credit Union Savings
- ☐ Dentist
- ☐ Diet Program
- ☐ Disability Income
- ☐ Doctor
- ☐ Domestic Help
- ☐ Education Expenses
- ☐ Entertainment
- ☐ Exercise Programs
- ☐ Furniture and Decorating
- ☐ Grocery
- ☐ Hair Cuts
- ☐ Health Insurance
- ☐ Hobbies
- ☐ Home Electricity
- ☐ Home Gas Heating
- ☐ Homeowner Insurance
- ☐ Household Maintenance and Repair
- ☐ Income Taxes: Federal, State, and Local
- ☐ Lawn and Yard Care
- ☐ Legal Fees
- ☐ Lessons
- ☐ Life Insurance
- ☐ Loans
- ☐ Magazines and Books
- ☐ Medicines and Vitamins
- ☐ Mortgage Payments
- ☐ Mutual Funds
- ☐ Newspapers

- ☐ Optician and Glasses
- ☐ Outside Meals
- ☐ Parking and Tolls
- ☐ Payroll Deductions
- ☐ Personal Care, Make-up
- ☐ Personal Debts
- ☐ Pet Food and Toys
- ☐ Petty Cash
- ☐ Public Transportation
- ☐ Real Estate Taxes
- ☐ Recreation
- ☐ Recycling Service
- ☐ Rent
- ☐ Salon Appointments
- ☐ Spending Money
- ☐ Stocks and Bonds
- ☐ Telephone
- ☐ Vacation Home
- ☐ Vacations
- ☐ Vehicle Gas and Oil
- ☐ Vehicle Insurance
- ☐ Vehicle License
- ☐ Vehicle Maintenance and Repair
- ☐ Veterinary
- ☐ Waste Removal
- ☐ Water

Index

"$" Account
    defined, 33
    gifts, bonuses, refunds, raises,
        34, 47, 84
    how much spending money
        you have, 34, 37
    initial sheet for example family
        budget, 63
    similarity to Monitored Budget
        Account, 47, 49
    spending unbudgeted money,
        34, 69, 72–73
    transferring money, 128–30

A

account transfers. *See* transferring
    money
automatic payments, 59, 78
    benefits of, 162–63
    defined, 162
    setting up, 163

B

bills
    annual, semi-annual, 41, 42
    auto-pay. *See* automatic
        payments
    due dates, 58, 61
    more or less the same from
        month to month, 44
    no exact due date, 60
    no past history, 46
    pay online, 150
    payment styles, 135
    prior to start of budget, 75–78

receiving refunds. *See* "$"
    Account
same from month to month, 42
varying widely from month to
    month, 47
bonuses. *See* "$" Account
Bounded Budget Item
    choosing amount, 44–46
    defined, 44
    entering in the Master Budget
        Sheet, 84–86
    examples of, 44–47
    receiveing refunds. *See* "$"
        Account
budget adjustments
    changes to budget, 125–28
    changes to budget amount, 44
budget plan
    utility company, 51, 52
budgeting
    benefits, 2–4
    communication tool with
        family, 17
    creating a list of expenses. *See*
        expenses
    defined, 2, 39
    envelope method, 7, 137
    for a "fun" item, 17
    goals, 156–58
    list-in-the-pocket method, 9
    myths, 4–6
    on computers. *See* computers
    repayment of loans. *See* loans
    retirement. *See* retirement
    self-improvement, 165–66
    the real secret, 168
    using cash, 136–38

using credit cards, 138–45. *See*
   credit cards
using exact amounts, 43
when to start?, 63
wish list method, 8
BudgetYes
   answers to exercises, 91–94
   bills prior to start of budget,
      75–78
   changes to your budget. *See*
      budget adjustments
   exercises, 89–90
   handling raises and bonuses,
      130
   how much spending money do
      you have, 37
   how to set it up, 58–61
   how to start the budget, 63–64
   Income Event, 20
   initial sheets for example family
      budget, 61–63
   Magnificent Triple, 131–32
   Master Budget Sheet, 27–30
   Monitored Budget Account, 49
   overlay for investment
      accounts, 145–46
   overlay for your checking
      account, 10, 67, 109
   overview, 9–11
   pay-ahead scheme, 52
   processing your checking
      account statement, 78–80
   the real secret, 168
   using a database program, 154
   using a spreadsheet, 154
   using cash, 136–38
   using computers. *See* computers
   using credit cards, 138–45. *See*
      credit cards
BudgetYes Philosophy
   defined, 11

C

cash, 136–38
changes to your budget. *See*
   budget adjustments
checking account
   adding interest payment to "$"
      Account, 79
   BudgetYes provides an overlay
      of your balance, 10
   interest bearing, 13
   minimum balance requirement,
      66
   processing your statement, 78–
      80
computers
   advantages of budgeting on,
      149–51
   commercial software, 151–54
   database programs, 154
   difference between BudgetYes
      and commercial software,
      152–53
   for investment management,
      151
   spreadsheets, 154
credit cards, 138–45
   benefits, 138
   control purchases with a
      Monitored Budget Account,
      139, 143–45
   handling purchases under
      BudgetYes, 141–45
   how to select cards, 141
   interest, 138
   using premiums and bonuses to
      your advantage, 143
   who should (not) use them?,
      138–40

D

database programs, 154
deductions
    by employer, 56

E

emergency fund, 34
envelope method, 7
    combined with BudgetYes, 137
example family budget
    scenario, 56
    setting up initial BudgetYes
        sheets, 61–63
expenses
    organizing, 15–16
    selecting items to budget for,
        16–18, 57

G

gifts. *See* "$" Account
goals, 156–58
grocery. *See* Monitored Budget
    Account

I

Income Event
    defined, 20
    distributing expenses across
        multiple Income Events, 58–
        61
    how to enter on Master Budget
        Sheet, 29–30, 67–71
    income versus bonuses, 25
    normalizing, 20–25, 147–48
    processing multiple Income
        Events per month, 82–84
    who needs to normalize, 21,
        147

initializing your budget, 63
interest
    bearing checking account, 13
    credit card, 138
    earning, 49
    payments, 79

L

list-in-the-pocket budgeting
    method, 9
loans
    repayment, 163–64

M

Magnificent Triple, 101, 131–32
    defined, 132
Master Budget Sheet, 27–30
    changes to your budget. *See*
        budget adjustments
    defined, 27
    how to enter data (spend
        money!), 30–32
    how to enter Income Event,
        29–30
    initial sheets for example family
        budget, 61–63
    marking a Bounded Budget
        Item, 84–87. *See* Bounded
        Budget Item
    marking a Monitored Budget
        Item, 80–82. *See* Monitored
        Budget Item
    marking a Simple Budget Item,
        73–75. *See* Simple Budget
        Item
    transferring money to a
        Monitored Budget Account,
        71
Monitored Budget Account

account transfers. *See*
    transferring money
defined, 49
earning interest, 49
example Grocery, 70
example Natural Gas, 80
example of, 49, 62
for credit card purchases, 143–
    45
for investment accounts, 145–
    46
initial sheets for example family
    budget, 62
normalize irregular income,
    147–48
set up, 50
similiarity to "$" Account, 49
transferring money from a
    Master Budget Sheet, 71
Monitored Budget Item
    choosing amount, 51–53
    defined, 48
    entering in the Master Budget
        Sheet, 80–82
    examples of, 80–82, 62
myths about budgeting, 4–6

N

natural gas. *See* Monitored Budget
    Account
normalize, 20–25
    by using BudgetYes, 24, 147–48
    by using savings and checking
        acount together, 22
    defined, 21

O

organizing expenses. *See* expenses
organizing records. *See* records
overlay

checking account, 10, 34, 66,
    109
investment accounts, 145–46

P

pay
    frequency, 21, 26, 131, 148
    types of, 19
payday. *See* Income Event
    triple pay. *See* Magnificent
        Triple
payments
    automatic. *See* automatic
        payments
    using cash. *See* cash
    using credit cards. *See* credit
        cards
pre-tax retirement savings plan, 56

R

raises. *See* "$" Account
reconciling, 43, 101, 128, 146
    defined, 110
    errors, 117–21
    example of, 111–17
    four steps, 111
    how frequently should you?,
        123–24
records
    organizing financial papers, 18
    where to store them, 18
refunds. *See* "$" Account
retirement, 159–61
    employer-provided pre-tax
        savings plan, 56
    power of compound interest,
        159

S

safe-deposit box
for important original documents,
    18
Simple Budget Item
    defined, 40
    entering in the Master Budget
        Sheet, 73–75
    example of, 73–75, 84
software. *See* computers
spending unbudgeted money. *See*
    "$" Account
spreadsheets, 154
starting your budget, 63–64

T

telephone bill, 75
transferring money
    between two Monitored
        Budget Accounts, 128–30
    from a Master Budget Sheet,
        71, 130
triple pay. *See* Magnificent Triple

U

utility company budget plan, 51,
    52

W

wish list budgeting method, 8

Filing Cabinet:
A place to lose
things
alphabetically.

Author Unknown

About the Authors

Jane E. Chidester and **John L. Macko** have been helping people get control of their money with BudgetYes seminars since 1992. This book grew out of the requests of their seminar attendees who wanted to be able to refer back to key points of the program and share the system with others. BudgetYes represents the culmination of over fifteen years of refinement based on real life experience and a wealth of different reviewers and perspectives.

Jane and John have been just one of the harmonious success stories of the BudgetYes system. Not only have they handled their finances very compatibly for their decade-long honeymoon, but also they are still married after working on this book together for over three years! ☺

Their interests include traveling, walking, hiking, biking, skiing, computers, and Disney.

* Photo Credit: Penny Adams, Adler House Photography

BudgetYes! Questionnaire

Please help! We'd love to know your thoughts! If we make a change in the next edition based on your comments, we'll list you in our Acknowledgments section. ☺ *If you have a financial success story, please share it with us!*

Comments about the structure of the book (layout, readability, price)?

Did you, or do you intend to, implement the BudgetYes system?

Did this book help you? Why or Why Not?

Send to address on back of page.

Other Comments?

❑   Please check if we may quote any of your comments in our promotions.

Your Name:

Street Address:

City, State:

Zip Code:

Phone Number   (   )

Send to:

**Tulip Tree Press
P.O. Box 1495-2
Powell, OH 43065**

Thank You!

BudgetYes! Order Form

Price of *BudgetYes!*: $19.95
Ohio Sales Tax: Ohio Residents Only: 5.75%
Shipping: $4.00
Satisfaction: 100% Guaranteed ☺

Your Name: _____
Street Address: _____
City, State _____
Zip Code: _____

Ship To (if different): _____
Street Address: _____
City, State _____
Zip Code _____

Please allow 4-6 weeks for delivery.

Number of Books: [＿＿] Sub-Total: _____

Ohio Sales Tax ($1.15 per book): _____

Shipping: $4.00

Total Price: _____

Send Form and Check to:

TULIPTREE
·P·R·E·S·S·

Tulip Tree Press
P.O. Box 1495-2
Powell, OH 43065

Thank You!

BudgetYes! Order Form

Price of *BudgetYes!*: $19.95
Ohio Sales Tax: Ohio Residents Only: 5.75%
Shipping: $4.00
Satisfaction: 100% Guaranteed ☺

Your Name: _____
Street Address: _____
City, State _____
Zip Code: _____

Ship To (if different): _____
Street Address: _____
City, State _____
Zip Code _____

Please allow 4-6 weeks for delivery.

Number of Books: [   ]   Sub-Total: _____

Ohio Sales Tax ($1.15 per book): _____

Shipping: $4.00

Total Price: _____

Send Form and Check to:

Tulip Tree Press
P.O. Box 1495-2
Powell, OH 43065

Thank You!